REREADING LITERATURE
Virginia Woolf

REREADING LITERATURE
General Editor: Terry Eagleton

W. H. Auden
Stan Smith

William Blake
Edward Larrissy

Emily Brontë
James H. Kavanagh

Geoffrey Chaucer
Stephen Knight

Charles Dickens
Steven Connor

Ben Jonson
Peter Womack

Alexander Pope
Laura Brown

William Shakespeare
Terry Eagleton

Alfred Tennyson
Alan Sinfield

Virginia Woolf
Rachel Bowlby

Virginia Woolf
Feminist Destinations

Rachel Bowlby

Basil Blackwell

First published 1988

Basil Blackwell Ltd
108 Cowley Road, Oxford, OX4 1JF, UK

Basil Blackwell Inc.
432 Park Avenue South, Suite 1503
New York, NY 10016, USA

British Library Cataloguing in Publication Data

Bowlby, Rachel
Virginia Woolf—(Rereading literature).
1. Woolf, Virginia—Criticism and interpretation
I. Title II. Series
823'.912 PR6045.072Z/
ISBN 0-631-15189-3
ISBN 0-631-15191-5

Library of Congress Cataloging in Publication Data

Bowlby, Rachel, 1957–
Virginia Woolf.
(Rereading literature)
Bibliography: p.
Includes index.
1. Woolf, Virginia, 1882–1941—Criticism and interpretation. I. Title. II. Series.
PR6045.072Z5615 1988 823'.912 87-30919
ISBN 0-631-15189-3
ISBN 0-631-15191-5 (pbk.)

Typeset in 11 on 12 pt Baskerville
by Opus, Oxford
Printed in Great Britain by Billing & Sons Ltd, Worcester

For Geoff

Contents

Editor's Preface

Virginia Woolf, as Rachel Bowlby points out in this study, is the only twentieth-century British woman writer to be taken seriously by critics of all casts. To celebrate her modernism while downplaying her feminism has been a familiar tactic of modern male critics, one which certain 'realist' feminists have ironically put into reverse. What Bowlby illuminatingly shows, however, is that none of these categories – modernist, feminist, realist – is at all stable within Woolf's own texts, which circulate them constantly in a whole set of alliances and antagonisms. If feminism is a far from unitary concept for feminist critics today, ranging as it does from affirmations of a natural but suppressed female difference to an insistence on the precariousness of all constructions of gender, from claims for an 'indigenous' female literary tradition to the question of a certain literary *mode* – then all of these positions, as Bowlby demonstrates, can already be found active in the works of a woman capable of writing in the very same essay that women writers should not think of their sex, and that they should 'think back through [their] mothers'. It is surely true also that the categories 'realism' and 'modernism' are perilous precisely because mutually complicit, as the latter ironically posits the former in the very act of transgressing it.

If the sex-changing, cross-dressing Orlando deeply troubles the assumption of fixed gender positions, cavalierly crossing the line from one identity to another, *To the Lighthouse* represents a darker insight into the woman's 'structurally untenable position' within male-dominated society, subtly undermining any complacently 'androgynous' ideal unity. *Mrs Dalloway*, in Bowlby's deft reading, is a rather more 'subjunctive' work, presenting us with the various possible destinies or identities at which women may or may not arrive, and gripped by a pervasive sense of ontological incertitude. *Jacob's Room, The Years* and *Between the Acts* take up these problematic questions of identity rather more temporally, as questions of historical change, biographical representation and the merging of fiction, language and reality in any historical construction. Such modernist interrogations of the possibility of a unified, linear, evolutionary history are not, as Bowlby argues, one 'aspect' of Woolf, as her feminism is another. On the contrary, that feminism is itself a way of viewing historical development and literary representation, a shrewd discernment that such apparently genderless matters are always sexually inflected. and it is in this constant double focusing, on sexual position and literary technique, on the structure of a text and the structure of a gendered self, that much of the strength of this lucid, intricate study lies.

Terry Eagleton

Acknowledgements

For their encouragement in the writing and for offering advice on various chapter drafts, I thank particularly Geoff Bennington, Laura Marcus, Jacqueline Rose and Alan Sinfield. Early versions of parts of the book were given as papers to audiences at the universities of Cardiff, Warwick and Sussex, at the University of California, Berkeley, and at McGill University, Montreal, and I learned much from the questions and comments in discussions afterwards. I should also like to thank Bet Inglis of Sussex University Library for her generous help.

Acknowledgement is made to the estate of Virginia Woolf and The Hogarth Press for permission to use extracts from the Woolf texts.

Abbreviations and Note on the Texts

All references to texts of Woolf are included within the main text, using abbreviations and editions as in the following list. The date given is that of the original publication.

VO	*The Voyage Out* London: Granada	1915
ND	*Night and Day* London: Granada	1919
JR	*Jacob's Room* London: Granada	1922
MD	*Mrs Dalloway* London: Granada	1925
TL	*To the Lighthouse* New York: Harcourt, Brace & World	1927
O	*Orlando* London: Granada	1928
ROO	*A Room of One's Own* London: Granada	1929
W	*The Waves* London: Granada	1931
Y	*The Years* London: Granada	1937
TG	*Three Guineas* New York: Harcourt, Brace & World	1938
RF	*Roger Fry: A Biography* London: Hogarth Press	1940
BA	*Between the Acts* New York: Harcourt, Brace, Jovanovich	1941
CE	*Collected Essays*, I-IV London: Chatto & Windus	1967
MB	*Moments of Being: Unpublished Autobiographical Writings* London: Granada	1976
P	*The Pargiters* New York: Harcourt, Brace, Jovanovich	1977

D *The Diary of Virginia Woolf, 1–5* Harmondsworth: Penguin 1977–84

The *Collected Essays* were edited by Leonard Woolf; *Moments of Being* by Jeanne Schulkind; *The Pargiters* by Mitchell A. Leaska; and the *Diaries* by Anne Olivier Bell, assisted for three of the volumes by Andrew McNeillie.

1 'We're Getting There': Woolf, Trains and the Destinations of Feminist Criticism

Trains, like women, are never on time. This is a truism of which it seems only fair to remind the reader, realizing that not everyone necessarily falls into the category of British Rail traveller or spectator of British television commercials. 'We're getting there' has been an advertising slogan utilized by British Rail to promise possible future efficiency in the form of timely arrivals at a destination; and the slogan derives any efficacity it might itself have in getting through to its destined audience by going against what it takes as a prevailing assumption on the public's part that British Rail doesn't, or won't, get there.

Given a question of trains, some of that public might perhaps be moved to make a connection with Saussure's example, renowned on certain academic networks, of the 8.45 p.m. express from Paris to Geneva and the issues of identity and difference which it raises.[1] In what sense might today's train, and the line it follows, be different from yesterday's? Others – or perhaps the same people – might go in the direction of Melanie Klein's pedagogical playing of trains with her young patient Dick, invited or pushed to identify the train with 'Daddy' and the station with his mother.[2] And at these points, 'We're getting there' arrives at or returns to the similarities or differences between trains and women, and the possible ends or destinations implied in speaking of 'feminist' writing and criticism. Where is feminism, or feminist theory, going, and what would constitute its 'arrival', the end of the 'movement'? Is the very idea of getting from *A* to *B* – or indeed from *A* to *Z* – necessarily bound up with masculine fantasies of linear progression that feminism should have no truck with?

Virginia Woolf's 1924 essay 'Mr Bennett and Mrs Brown' is a kind of literary Clapham Junction for the crossing and potential collision of questions of representation, history and sexual difference.[3] Taking as its starting point the subject of 'modern fiction', the essay is cast in narrative form. It tells the story of an unfinished third-class railway journey from the periphery to the centre of London involving a 'Mrs Brown' whose key, if marginal, position is well enough indicated: 'I believe', declares Woolf, 'that all novels begin with an old lady in the corner opposite' (*CE*, I: 324). Also present is a man called Mr Smith; the narrator, who represents herself as one of the passengers, uses the scene as a vehicle for discussing 'what novelists mean when they talk about character, what the impulse is that urges them so powerfully every now and then to embody their views in writing' (321). Woolf stresses the 'infinite variety of ways' that Mrs Brown could be represented or 'treated', according to the 'age, country or temperament' of the writer (325). Such differences are further signalled by the train's ambiguous status as a form of communication between two points, whether they be historical moments, novelistic conventions, the two sexes, the two ladies (who never speak to one another), or the writer and the readers to whom the communication of Mrs Brown is no straightforward matter. By the end of the journey, this question of forms of communication has coupled itself with that of historical change and how to represent it. What does it mean to travel from *A* to *B*, from Richmond to Waterloo, from the Edwardians to the Georgians, and perhaps from 'realism' to 'modernism'? And might it have something to do with a movement from Mr Bennett to Mrs Brown, or indeed to Mrs Woolf? A third type of issue breaks in here, as the passage from one literary or historical phase to the next seems to become inextricably involved with a contention about injustices and reparations to the old lady.

Within the context of the essay, the scene is set up to dislocate the tedious compilations of data associated, for

Woolf, with the pre-war Edwardian novelists. Wells, Bennett and Galsworthy are individually parodied via sardonic paraphrases of each one's likely narrative versions of the encounter on the train with the 'old lady in the corner opposite' (324) who hypothetically begins every novel. In this dispute, the old lady is up for grabs, caught between opposing constructions of her likely story or background, all of which, apparently, claim to have fixed her once and for all.

But much more is going on in the train than this initial retelling of Woolf's story would suggest. In addition to the problem of identifying the woman there is another line running through it, which is a thesis about the historical development and contemporary situation of the English novel. The infinite number of stories to which Mrs Brown might give rise would in this light appear to depend not so much on the static personal or national predilections of novelists as on the changing 'code' (334) or 'conventions' (330) of literary representation. In this framework, the Edwardians figure as a point of transition between nineteenth-century literature and whatever will supersede it. That something else is on the way is suggested both by 'the smashing and the crashing' (333–4) of the subsequent Georgian generation, and by the allegedly self-evident obsoleteness of Edwardian conventions or 'tools' (330) of factual realism.

It is surely no accident that the encounter with Mrs Brown takes place on a train. By this time, the imagery of public transport had become literally a commonplace for suggesting the repetitive and banal 'types' of realist fiction, as with the standardized 'man on the Clapham omnibus'. Woolf, on the contrary, alters the terms – by putting the novelist into the carriage with her subject, and by using the public space as a sign of strangeness rather than predictability. She also suggests, as we shall see, that the sexes of the participants are by no means a matter of indifference. Writers, characters, readers and the linguistic means of bringing about an interchange between them are radically shaken around in this suburban railway carriage which is at first sight such an unlikely setting for an argument *against* realism. Here, the theme of transport and movement makes way for the contrast with the stationary quality of the Edwardian writers' preoccupation with houses. The compartment does have some of the qualities of the domestic sitting room, but this only adds to its curiously ambivalent suspension half-way between two states, in this respect as in others. This is a public space superficially identical to a private one, so that the anonymity of the limited number of passengers is all the more significant from its contrast to the scene of intimacy it resembles.

Following another line, the train indicates a mobile rather than static or external position for the narrator. In fact, the train suggests several possible relations between observer and subject. There is the train passing, seen from elsewhere; there is what is seen from the train through the window, like a picture in motion; and there is the scene inside the railway compartment. All these positions will prove to be important in looking at Woolf's narratives; and it is also worth recalling here that trains at this period had no corridors, so that passengers were completely confined to their carriage while the train was between stations.[4]

In terms of literary history, Woolf's piece links the movement beyond Edwardian realism to a shift in consciousness which is hypothetically, if not arbitrarily, marked at a specific date. This is the famous and enigmatic pronouncement that 'in or about December, 1910, human character changed' (320). Here Woolf takes the line of historical determination as far as it will go, to a point where chronological precision practically becomes a caricature of this type of explanation. Her formula is an exasperated transposition of the blandness of factual records to the shock effect of a sensational headline or slogan. In the very form of the quasi-ludicrous specification, Woolf questions the possibility of anything like the confident ordering, listing and chronicling she associates with the Edwardians. It can never be more than provisional and retrospective, at least for the post-1910 mind, to posit a fixed position from which to view or analyse what might be seen as an event or a change in human society or consciousness.[5] But Woolf's provocatively sloganizing style could itself be linked to the alleged change in forms of communication and understanding: it could be compared to the 'skywriting' aeroplane advertisement in *Mrs Dalloway*; or to the need to mark a distinction between what she calls later in the essay the 'myriads of irrelevant and incongruous ideas' (323) which are constantly vying to make an impression.

Woolf continues, then, by stressing that her claim marks serious questions about historical change and its representation:

> I am not saying that one went out, as one might into a garden, and there saw that a rose had flowered, or that a hen had laid an egg. The change was not sudden and definite like that. But a change there was, nevertheless, and, since one must be arbitrary, let us date it about the year 1910.
>
> (*CE* I: 320)

It is neither a matter of the repeated cycles of nature – hens and flowers – nor of simple chronology – 1910, 1911, 1912. But the demarcation of an 'event', 'arbitrary' and approximate though it must be, is still an issue of some consequence. In this case – both a seemingly random 'example' and a test case on which all of history and history-writing will hang – it will not be a matter of discovering and then instantly transmitting the true nature of a transhistorical and eternal Mrs Brown, the natural woman hitherto unrepresented or distorted in fiction and now to be seen at last blooming in her corner. Nor will it be a matter of Mrs Brown's presence on the train simply being noted, *à la* Bennett, as evidence of progressive female emancipation: before the war, Mrs Brown would have needed a protector and now she travels alone. Mrs Brown is neither a natural phenomenon nor a social statistic, and it is not yet clear what difference the fact of her being a woman might make.

To some extent, as the ambivalence of her use of the concept of 'convention' shows, the *terminus ad quem* for novel-writing is presupposed in the way the story is set up: Edwardian realism is considered by Woolf to be at once historically necessary and necessarily overtaken as only a first stop on the line: its 'conventions' are also said to be like those of a hostess 'bridging the gulf' with her 'unknown guest' (330), and never getting beyond what should be only preliminary chat about the weather. The objection to this as too simple is the starting point for Woolf's expository journey when she introduces Mrs Brown as standing for the problem she claims to be common to novelists at all times, of how to represent 'that overwhelming and peculiar impression' (323) produced by the unknown potential character:

> Myriads of irrelevant and incongruous ideas crowd into one's head on such occasions; one sees the person, one sees Mrs Brown, in the centre of all sorts of different scenes.
>
> (*CE* I: 323–24)

The prospective author does not sit in a neutral position surveying a knowable scene; rather, she is afflicted from outside by the 'myriads' of ideas which 'crowd' in without any principle of order or coherence, 'irrelevant and incongruous'. The language here can be related to the modernist 'stream' of consciousness – or perhaps it should rather be called a 'train' of thought – the 'fragments' and 'chaotic condition' of current literature then corresponding to or emanating from a chaotic, fragmented state of mind which has now taken over from the clearly marked boundaries and certainties of Edwardian stability. But such a change cannot be simply narrated as a movement from outer to inner; instead, as this sentence shows, it is a question of a different relationship between inside and outside in which the chaotic incoherence of mental 'ideas' is identified with the social 'crowd', and where the disturbing effect of the whole crowd is produced by 'that overwhelming and peculiar impression' (323) of the single old lady seen in the railway carriage.

The issue, then, is not so much one of ebbs and flows in the vitality of artistic conventions, despite Woolf's implicit use of an Arnoldian alternation between 'critical' and 'creative' periods of literary history. Rather, it involves a completely new representation of social and subjective experience. In terms of writing, it is only the striking claim which will jolt the reader amid such a barrage of chaotic impressions. At the end of her lecture, Woolf makes an explicit identification between writer and reader as fellow observers of the mysterious Mrs Brown:

> For she is just as visible to you who remain silent as to us who tell stories about her. In the course of your daily life this past week you have had far stranger and more interesting experiences than the one I have tried to describe. You have overheard scraps of talk that filled you with amazement. You have gone to bed at night bewildered by the complexity of your feelings. In one day thousands of ideas have coursed through your brains; thousands of emotions have met, collided and disappeared in astonishing disorder.
>
> (*CE* I: 336)

Mrs Brown now moves on from being just a symbol of literary character. Here she becomes a figure for the confusion and 'complexity' of a 'daily life' represented as the source of the internal 'disorder' of the 'thousands of ideas' to which, like her, it gives rise. There is 'amazement' and unfamiliarity in the most everyday experiences, in the fragmentary, anonymous quality of the 'overheard scraps of talk'. Inner and outer, seer and seen, psychic and social, can in no way be represented apart.

Despite this engagement with the representation of personal experience as a social and historical question, Woolf has often been criticized or dismissed for a presumed elitism in her linguistic complexity, or a snobbish indifference to or ignorance of the details of ordinary life to which the novelists from which she distinguishes herself devoted such minute attention. In this kind of argument, she is set up as the aristocratic lady whose leisure and income enabled her to retreat into a private, self-contained haven whence to expatiate on the beauties of Art and the delicate contents of her self-absorbed mind. There are, certainly, many moments in Woolf's writing where it is not difficult to understand the possible grounds for such a case. In this essay, for instance, the reader is encouraged to seek substantiation for the alleged change in human character by reference to the case of 'one's cook' (320). There are assumptions in that 'one's' which grate now in the same way as most uses of the masculine as a general pronoun by someone writing after the mid-1970s.

If the problem is granted to be one involving changing conventions of writing and changing assumptions of readership, then the objection can only be sustained if the writer is imagined to be some transcendentally omni-egalitarian consciousness, not only ahead of her time but outside time altogether. But it is usually the consciously 'historical' critic who makes this type of criticism, ironically working from idealist, ahistorical assumptions about the practice of authorship which would be rejected immediately in other contexts. In this particular example, in fact, not only is the question of historical change the actual theme of Woolf's argument, but it is the rise of the cook – upstairs from the 'lower depths' of the Victorian cellar to the reading of newspapers and the borrowing of hats – which is given as a 'homely illustration' of 'the power of the human race to change' (320).[6]

It is precisely around this question of the changing place of women that Woolf's objections to the Edwardian writers become most insistent. 'How shall I begin to describe this woman's character?' she asks:

> And they said: 'Begin by saying that her father kept a shop in Harrogate. Ascertain the rent. Ascertain the wages of shop assistants in the year 1878. Discover what her mother died of. Describe cancer. Describe calico. Describe – ' But I cried: 'Stop! Stop!' And I regret to say that I threw that ugly, that clumsy, that incongruous tool out of the window.
>
> (*CE* I: 332)

As Woolf in desperation calls a halt to the train, the over-extended conversational formalities of the Edwardian novelist-as-hostess have taken on the far less genteel appearance of an ugly, clumsy 'tool'.[7] Like the 'man's sentence' in *A Room of One's Own*, it is clearly 'unsuited for a woman's use' (*ROO*, 73), and like the 'awkward break' Woolf there identifies (*ROO*, 66) in the text of *Jane Eyre*, and then herself repeats by breaking off the quotation, 'Stop! Stop!' is an angry refusal of any continuity between the men's way of approaching Mrs Brown and her own.

Woolf pulls the communication cord on Edwardian certainties in no uncertain terms, exposing the masculine force that lies behind the seemingly neutral Edwardian equipment. The overtones here of rape are foregrounded even more strongly within the main line of the story, where the narrator who enters the compartment comes upon what appears to be a violent scene between Mr Smith and Mrs Brown: 'It was plain . . . that he had some power over her which he was exerting disagreeably. . . . Obviously against her will she was in Mr Smith's hands' (*CE*, I: 322–3). And then, following the man's abrupt departure at Clapham Junction: 'He had got what he wanted, but he was ashamed of himself' (323).

Given the title of the essay, which would not lead the reader to expect a story about a Mr Smith, it is not hard to see in the 'bullying, menacing' Mr Smith (323) a reference to Mr Bennett. As Mrs Brown also represents novelistic character in general, Woolf's narrating of her own entry into the train becomes all the more significant: 'I had the strange and uncomfortable feeling that I was interrupting' (321). What she turns out to imagine herself interrupting is this spectacle of suppressed violence, perpetrated by a man against a woman, over a matter having to do with the signing away of property. This situation is then plotted on to the running question about the transition or break between one literary period and the next, when the old lady starts later on to complain at her own misrepresentation: 'There was Mrs Brown protesting that she was different, quite different, from what people made out, and luring the novelist to her rescue' (333).

Mrs Brown's protest, echoing Woolf's own 'Stop! Stop!' then leads to an explicit connection between the inadequacy of literary tools and the rescue of the woman:

> At whatever cost to life, limb, and damage to valuable property Mrs Brown must be rescued, expressed, and set in her high relations to the world before the train stopped and she disappeared for ever. And so the smashing and the crashing began.
>
> (*CE*, I: 333–4)

It might seem that Mrs Woolf's fortunate interruption will suffice to secure the reappraisal and rise of the maligned and molested Mrs Brown, as the two ladies settle down comfortably at last, with Mr Smith and his tools safely out of the way, reading and writing in a railway carriage of their own. But things do not advance so rapidly. The pressing need for Mrs Brown's rescue has so far only produced 'the smashing and the crashing' of the Georgians which sounds no different from the earlier antics of Mr Smith's incursions on Mrs Brown: 'He banged. He slammed. His dripping umbrella made a pool in the hall' (324). With a certain matronly disapproval, Woolf likens the behaviour of the new writers to the rebelliousness of little boys rolling in the mud as a resistance to genteel constraints (334).

Woolf's suspicions here lead her to mark the present time as only a station *en route* to a prospective arrival at new conventions where Mrs Brown will be decently treated. But in discussing why change should proceed so slowly, she raises another question, wheeling on yet another 'strange travelling companion' in the form of that 'suggestible and docile creature', the public (332). And here, once again, her illustration has to do with the representation of sexual difference:

> If you say to the public with sufficient conviction: 'All women have tails, and all men humps,' it will actually learn to see women with tails and men with humps, and will think it very revolutionary and probably improper if you say: 'Nonsense. Monkeys have tails and camels humps. But men and women have brains, and they have hearts; they think and they feel,' – that will seem to it a bad joke, and an improper one into the bargain.
>
> (*CE*, I: 332–33)

In this full-blown send-up of conventional representations, what the 'docile' public finds unacceptable is the alteration of what is already a reversal of the symbolic norm, that women have humps and men tails. But this parody is reinforced by a parody of symbolic significance itself, in the literalizing of the humps and tails; and the whole question of the difference of the sexes is deflected onto the distinction of power and intelligence that supposedly operates between the meaning-making writers and their obtuse but potentially stubborn public, a neutral 'creature' or 'it'.

Sexual difference may, then, mean nothing, or something 'quite different', in the end or the future; but in the meantime it is the source both of the gravest injustice, in the mistaking of Mrs Brown, and of the greatest resistance to change on the part of a convention-bound public. Mrs Brown's claim to be 'different, quite different from what people made out' suspends the conclusion of her story by withholding a positive identification of what she might be, and establishing the issue as having to do with representational conventions. Her difference is not necessarily that of absolute uniqueness or that of Woman from Man in some absolute sense; it is difference *from* the way she is presently dealt with.

As the train makes its way from Richmond to Waterloo, this question of sexual difference has come, at least in this interested reconstruction of the journey, to occupy a place of privilege. It seems clear that by or about the 1920s, questions of possible modifications in 'human character' have come to formulate themselves in terms of male and female character and their different lines of development. While at one level the conventions of Edwardian realism are mocked as merely anachronistic or as meaningless, like the superficialities of polite hostesses, at another their tools are associated with a violence that borders on the threat of rape. The 'illustrations' in this essay – Mrs Brown herself; 'one's cook' and 'the power of the human race to change'; women with humps instead of tails – all turn out to have to do with women or sexual difference, and to link themselves into a miniature narrative or series of questions about the representation of woman and her place: from traditional representations of the fictitious old lady, through protestations of equal rights and difference from 'what they made out', to a parody of the social implications of male and female.

Woolf's third-class railway compartment has maintained its place as a *locus classicus* for discussions of the journey from realism and modernism as hypothetical stops on the line of literary history, or as general labels for alternative types of literary representation. Recently, this debate has become linked with feminist questions, with the possible move from

Mr Bennett to Mrs Brown as writers and with demands that the real Mrs Brown stand up, or sit down, not so much as 'character' or 'human life' in general, but as a woman. Pinning her down as a textual or sexual being, getting her to show the valid ticket of her twentieth-century identity, has become a major preoccupation. And the venerable old lady in the corner has come to look not a little like the figure of Mrs Woolf herself.

For it would seem that Woolf, like Mrs Brown, has become an 'exemplary' character – and exemplary in paradoxical ways. Woolf is the only twentieth-century British woman writer who is taken seriously by critics of all casts. Whether she is seen to fit in with or to subvert what the critic identifies as established literary standards, and depending on whether subversion or conformity is the criterion of value, Woolf is vehemently celebrated or denounced from all sides. Among feminist critics who approve her work, she is seen as exemplary both in the sense of exceptional – a *unique* heroine, a foremother, a figurehead – and as an example, in some way representative or typical of something called 'women's writing'. Among those who dislike her work, it is taken as not matching up to the criteria of women's writing, but fitting in all too well with the patriarchal norms, literary or social, to which authentic women's writing should by definition be opposed.

The issues in feminist criticism are related to the overt concerns of 'Mr Bennett and Mrs Brown': in particular, to what is at stake in the recent privileging of modernism because it brings into the foreground questions of language and representation. One strand of feminist criticism takes its cue from this model, positing women's writing as the principal locus of the undermining of realist conventions identified as masculine. Another strand, working with broadly 'realist' assumptions, takes 'women's writing' to describe a female experience hitherto devalorized, if not wholly banished, by the institutional or more general constraints implied by a patriarchal society. In the 'exemplary' case of Virginia Woolf – the woman writer *par excellence* and, at the same time, a test case for women's writing in general – this has led to various different types of criticism. She is celebrated as a modernist breaking with formal literary conventions, and thereby also with the normative structures of patriarchal – or phallocentric – language; she is also celebrated as a realist, by appeal to her authentic description of women's lives and experiences, and her commitment to the end of patriarchal society. At the same time, Woolf is also attacked from both these standpoints: as not realist enough (too much Bloomsbury aestheticism) or as not modernist enough (always falling back into a nostalgic desire for unities rather than radical breaks). Woolf has been confidently situated in all four categories, which then signals the fact that what goes on in her writing, and in particular what goes on in the famous railway carriage, is strikingly amenable to compartmentalization; but also that it doesn't easily stay put.

There is also the question of biography. On the one hand there are the legends of Bloomsbury and the privileged upbringing in a family where genial Victorian men of letters were always dropping in for tea. On the other hand there is the work with women's organizations, the lecturing to working-class women, the membership of a Sussex village Labour Party. Bloomsbury snob versus socialist feminist, by an easy enough transposition. Apart from the public persona, there is Woolf's personal legend, which leaves little to be desired or dreaded in the way of striking characterization. Childhood seduction, madness, confinement, frigidity, anorexia, lesbianism, suicide: in the very extremity of its outlines, the tale can become either a demonstration of common female oppression – the norm revealed at its outer edges – or proof of her exceptional status. In her oddness or in her representativeness, Virginia Woolf is always treated as a 'case'. Here again, with the woman as with her writing – and the two are rarely separated – it is the problem of the 'exemplary'. For her advocates, either the extraordinary nature of Woolf's life is what makes her distinctive, or its typicality is what makes her writing a woman's. For her detractors, Woolf's peculiarities mar her work and disqualify her from writing as a woman, or else her all too normal experiences confine her work within 'womanly' limits which cannot achieve the status of art.

It will be apparent from all this not only that Woolf is considered worthy of a formidable quantity of critical attention, but that the criticism frequently takes the form of violent attack or defence – of Virginia Woolf herself, of what she wrote, or (most often) of some nebulous fusion of the two. And somehow the question of identifying the real nature of Woolf gets bound up with identifying the real nature of woman, or literature, or feminism, or feminist literature. Like the Bible, Woolf's texts provide ample support for almost any position; she is taken to hold the key to the meaning of life and the proper nature of woman; she is the object of both veneration and vehement hatred; and like the Bible too, she is sometimes merely treated as 'literature'.

Uncannily enough, the 'Mr Bennett and Mrs Brown' essay seems to prefigure the fate of Woolf herself. 'I shall never know what became of her', Woolf says of Mrs Brown (324); but it is as if Woolf herself has since become nothing else than the all-purpose 'exemplary' figure of Mrs Brown, source of an endless variety of treatments and mistreatments and calling forth the most diverse and zealous critics and defenders, all eager to put her in her place, high or low, and to save her from those who have put her somewhere else. To take a recent example, Toril Moi's influential *Sexual/Textual Politics* on the present state of feminist criticism opens with a chapter on Woolf as a natural starting point for any discussion of this issue. Arguing against the realist assumptions of feminist critics of Woolf who object that she does not provide enough images of strong women, Moi then goes on to say that 'the major drawback of this approach is that it proves incapable of appropriating for feminism the work of the greatest British woman writer of this century'.[8] There is a possible tension here between the given absolute status of the greatest writer, and the criterion of utility, 'for feminism'; while 'appropriating' could sound not unlike what Mr Bennett *et al.* did to Mrs Brown – all the more ironically, in light of the fact that this section of the chapter is entitled 'Rescuing Woolf for feminist politics'.

Clearly, the Mrs Brown question does not easily go away. But I am not suggesting that it is possible or desirable to stop 'appropriating', 'rescuing', or even mildly mistreating 'Virginia Woolf', who says herself at the end of her essay on 'Modern Fiction': 'If we can imagine the art of fiction come alive and standing in our midst, she would undoubtedly bid us break her and bully her, as well as honour and love her, for so her youth is renewed and her sovereignty assured' (*CE*, II: 110). In saying that the (inconclusive) answers to almost all generalizing questions about 'woman', 'literature' and the rest are already anticipated by Woolf – in the 'Mrs Brown' essay and others, and above all, as we shall see in the next chapter, in *A Room of One's Own*, where she moves through just about all the positions that have subsequently been attributed to her as definite stances – I am, of course, only repeating the gesture of deification; but then it is not so easy to step out of this particular railway carriage.

To appropriate Toril Moi's suggestive link in my turn: it seems to me that the interest of Woolf's writing is to be found precisely in the juxtaposition Moi proposes between Woolf's literary achievement and her feminist questions. As in 'Mr Bennett and Mrs Brown', issues of literary representation, historical narrative and sexual difference are inseparable throughout Woolf's work. She insists upon the difficulty of distinguishing the question of what constitutes a plausible story, historical or biographical, from the question of what constitutes the difference of men and women. Sometimes her concern is more to dissect the presuppositions of received forms of representation, and sometimes it is more to argue from the given state of those forms, taking them as 'read'. Sometimes, that is, she analyses the railway compartment in all its contingency, showing the unfounded nature of its claim to normality; and at other times, she considers the compartment as it is, recognizing but disputing the sexually differentiated terms of travel it imposes, and asking where it may go from here.

In the chapters that follow, I try to show that it is precisely in her insistence on the sexual inflection of all questions of historical understanding and literary representation that Woolf is a feminist writer. She constantly associates certainty and conventionality with a complacent masculinity which she sees as setting the norms for models of individual and historical development. It makes sense, then, that it will be from the woman in the corner of the railway compartment – or the woman not synchronized with the time of the train – that the most fruitful and troubling questions will be posed, and that new lines may emerge. But given that Woolf is engaged in questioning the very notion of straightforward directions and known destinations, it is not clear what those lines will be, or where they will go; nor what a woman may look like, 'if and when' she has succeeded in changing the conditions of travel and the present timetable.

2 The Trained Mind

> I am almost sure, I said to myself, that Mary Carmichael is playing a trick on us. For I feel as one feels on a switchback railway when the car, instead of sinking, as one had been led to expect, swerves up again. Mary is tampering with the expected sequence. First she broke the sentence; now she has broken the sequence.
>
> (*ROO*, 78)

'But' is the first word of *A Room of One's Own*: a beginning against the conventions of 'what one had been led to expect' for Woolf the invited lecturer on 'Women and Fiction', as much as for the hypothetical new woman novelist, Mary Carmichael. Starting *in medias res*, as if a conversation had been going on already, Woolf's 'but' indicates, first of all, that the topic cannot be addressed from some place of absolute innocence: a story involving women and fiction in various complicated ways has been under way for quite some time (for the duration of written history, at least), and it would be utopian to imagine that it might be possible to discuss such a matter in abstract or ideal terms. Hence, as in 'Mr Bennett and Mrs Brown', a general question immediately takes a narrative turn, as Woolf moves – or is she just 'playing a trick'? – from theory to the fictional ramble through 'Oxbridge', London, the British Museum and through many byways of literary history, in an exploration where '"I" is only a convenient term for somebody who has no real being' (*ROO*, 6).

Secondly, the unconventional opening represents a provocative interruption of the discourse in progress. Like Mary Carmichael's 'tampering with the expected sequence' and with the norms of syntax, it represents a kind of 'butting in'. This has ramifications or branch lines throughout the text, as we shall see. On what, exactly, does 'Woolf' butt in, and does she do so only in so far as she is excluded from it? If it is as a woman that she interrupts something conceived as occupied or dominated by men, does she anticipate a future alteration of the terms on which that differential – between men and women, between the insiders and the outsiders – has operated so far?

Many different suggestions appear in the course of *A Room* for what is, or what makes, the difference between men and women, and the differences of men's and women's writing. Though Woolf (or rather Woolf's narrator, her 'convenient' I) settles for none in particular, some of them are now influential models for thinking about women and writing – or about Woolf – in their own right. While they can be broadly subsumed under the headings of 'historical' and 'psychological' – as having to do with social constraints or with possibly universal forms of psychic organization – part of their interest lies in the ways that in Woolf's analyses such divisions are themselves rendered more complicated, and altered by the ways that they turn out to impinge upon each other.

Materials

In an overtly historical mode, Woolf alludes to what she calls the 'material' conditions of writing. It is fallacious, she says, to think of Shakespeare as if he dropped from the sky: great works of literature

> are not spun in mid-air by incorporeal creatures, but are the work of suffering human beings, and are attached to grossly material things, like health and money and the houses we live in.
>
> (*ROO*, 41)

Owing to their lack of property and education, as well as to constraints on their freedom of movement and to demands on their time for other purposes, women have not been in a position to spin the particular substance of which Shakespeare's *oeuvre* is Woolf's favourite example: and Woolf cites the imaginary representative case of 'Shakespeare's sister' endowed with gifts equal to her brother's but unable, because of the position of women at the time, to make anything of them.[1]

But as compared with other professions, the material resources for writing are much easier to obtain. In another of her lectures of this period, 'Professions for Women', Woolf matter-of-factly points out that 'for ten and sixpence one can buy paper enough to write all the plays of Shakespeare' (*CE*, II: 284).[2] Joined with the fact that writing could just about be done, as it was by Jane Austen, in 'the common sitting-room' (*ROO*, 108), as opposed to a room and time of one's own, this accounts partly for why writing for money should have been so widely engaged in by women without material support from the conventional (male) quarters for themselves or for their dependants, once Aphra Behn and her followers had established the precedent.

Outsiders

The apparent simplicity of this factual enumeration of 'material' conditions already implies a further question about why women should have had less money or not have engaged in the same professional activities as men. Here a structural rather than statistical description comes into play. Woolf refers, in this text as in others, to British society as a 'patriarchy'. The use of this term indicates a hierarchical division of ruled and rulers, with 'fathers' providing the pivotal category. Whereas sons will inherit and mothers be honoured, daughters in this arrangement are not easily put in their place, except in that their place is one of exclusion from any position of authority. Woolf's references in *Three Guineas* to the non-place of 'the daughters of educated men' lead to the development of her proposal of a 'Society of Outsiders'. Such a position is adumbrated in *A Room* in the stories of the various exclusions to which the narrator is subjected in her wanderings round 'Oxbridge'. Having been shooed off for trespassing on the grass and debarred from entering the library, 'I thought how unpleasant it is to be locked out; and I thought how it is worse perhaps to be locked in' (*ROO*, 24).

It is thus that a position outside might turn out to hold more possibilities for forms of activity or reasoning ruled out a priori for those who have to maintain the proprieties of the insider group. Woolf's narrator is full of scorn and mockery for the stereotyped personifications of patriarchal conventions who don their gowns and their furs to parade an unswerving conformity to whatever institution it may be: 'As I leant against the wall the University indeed seemed a sanctuary in which are preserved rare types which would soon be obsolete if left to fight for existence on the pavement of the Strand' (10). Elsewhere – in London, in *Three Guineas*, for instance – the 'procession' of masculine tradition is less readily dismissed as a provincial anachronism, and the question becomes that of whether the hitherto excluded woman should want or attempt to join it (*TG*, 60–2).

Trespassing

> Instantly a man's figure rose to intercept me. Nor did I at first understand that the gesticulations of a curious-looking object, in a cut-away coat and evening shirt, were aimed at me. His face expressed horror and indignation. Instinct rather than reason came to my help; he was a Beadle; I was a woman. This was the turf; there was the path.
>
> (*ROO*, 7)

The walk through 'Oxbridge' approaches an allegory of the banning of women from the citadels of masculine authority, all the more effective for its deployment of the imagery of territorial demarcations. The colleges which do not admit women symbolize the male monopoly on every aspect of cultural authority.[3] In *Three Guineas*, Woolf develops in more detail the arguments around the mutual reinforcement of the social institutions which combine to keep women out, and questions whether theirs is the kind of power in which women would like to participate. In *A Room*, she shows the poverty of the women's college as an inevitable effect of the centuries of patriarchal control of the 'material' supports of such institutions.

> The most transient visitor to this planet, I thought, who picked up this paper could not fail to be aware, even from this scattered testimony, that England is under the rule of a patriarchy. Nobody in their senses could fail to detect the dominance of the professor. His was the power and the money and the influence. He was the proprietor of the paper and its editor and sub-editor. He was the Foreign Secretary and the Judge. He was the cricketer; he owned the racehorses and the yachts. He was the director of the company that pays two hundred per cent to its shareholders. He left millions to charities and colleges that were ruled by himself.
>
> (*ROO*, 33–4)

Woolf is thus quite unequivocal about the kind of social power that is at stake in the marking of different values and differential access to the public use of language. The terms are absolutely set out ('His was the power') and absolutely fixed according to the lines of gender: what is 'his' must not be hers.

It is one thing to name this power of exclusion and control 'patriarchy': Woolf can offer no rational explanation for such a thorough separation of functions between the sexes. Hence the exposure of the arbitrariness of the division: the opposition between 'Beadle' and 'woman' is enough to constitute a difference of which Woolf's narrator is in no more doubt than the 'curious-looking object' which rises up to intercept her movements. He, or it, butts in on the rumination about 'women and fiction' she has just begun, as if to call 'Halt!' to an illicit turn of thought. Against his authority she has no appeal; and she recognizes the meaning of his expression in a flash: by 'instinct' rather than reason. Since the law she recognizes is obviously cultural, this underlining of the received understanding of the difference between men's and women's ways of knowing – rationally or intuitively – then operates as its parodic undermining.

Its very pretension to exclusiveness seems to imply that male power is always under threat. The Beadle's response to the woman's presence on the grass is anything but neutral: his 'horror and indignation' show that a woman who fails to abide by the law has roused in him a reaction that itself goes beyond the bounds of reason. Woolf's narrator settles down in the British Museum with an 'avalanche of books' (28) written by authors with 'no qualification save that they were not women' (29). It is as if there is a continuous and never completed effort on the part of man to keep woman in the place assigned to her by him: outside the precincts of representational power, defined, bounded, in a proliferation of heterogeneous characteristics which the narrator lists for her readers in a parody of the books' pseudo-scholarly procedures (29).

Impediments

Following the historical line of reasoning, the differential access to sites of social authority and prestige gives rise to different kinds of thinking. His 'training' (29) means that the middle- or upper-class male learns to regulate and organize his writing in a way that a Dorothy Osborne or a Duchess of Newcastle could not; while its institutional back-up means that 'the freedom of the mind' (61) is not constrained for him by the need to attend to 'material' concerns. It is this difference of material and educational means which accounts for the contrast between the culinary amenities of the men's and women's colleges at the start of *A Room*, the amply or meagrely nourished bodies of their respective inmates providing food for Woolf's thoughts about the 'two pictures, disjointed and disconnected' (20) of the history of their respective endowments: munificent and age-old in one case, lacking and barely begun in the other. Reproductive differences are cited as one major reason why women have been confined within the limits of the private sphere, and later on the childlessness of many of the women who have been successful writers is noted as significant.[4]

Describing the writing of nineteenth-century women novelists, Woolf's narrator identifies flaws which she attributes to this arbitrary and historically contingent state of affairs. Charlotte Brontë's achievement is marred because: 'She will write in a rage where she should write calmly. . . . She is at war with her lot. How could she help but die young, cramped and thwarted?' (67). Such 'impediments' (65) in the writing – shared, for example, by a Lady Winchilsea 'bursting out' in her much earlier poetry 'in indignation against the position of women' (56) – are seen as socially induced: her 'defects' are 'those of her sex at the time' (67): 'It is clear that anger was tampering with the integrity of Charlotte Bronte the novelist. . . . She remembered that she had been starved of her proper due of experience – she had been made to stagnate in a parsonage mending stockings when she wanted to wander free over the world.' (70). These quotations imply that a novel and a writer should have 'integrity' and be free of 'anger' or 'indignation'. There is a horizon of wholeness and healthy development according to a given 'nature', in relation to which the failed novel or novelist will be dull ('stagnate') or 'cramped'.

A version of this model has become highly influential in recent feminist criticism. In Sandra Gilbert and Susan Gubar's *The Madwoman in the Attic* (1979), which deals in some detail with Charlotte Brontë's work, it is the constraints of patriarchal society and of a patriarchal literary tradition which are taken to inhibit what would otherwise be the free and full expression of the woman writer; division, in text or writer, is taken as a symptom of the ills produced by patriarchy.[5] Gilbert and Gubar demonstrate the ubiquity in nineteenth-century women's writing of metaphors and images of confinement, and representations of anger and madness. It is assumed that the male writers who currently wield the 'pen' that signifies cultural and literary authority do possess such personal and textual integration; in time, the woman writer may attain the same degree of autonomy.

The Difference of Value

> It is obvious that the values of women differ very often from the values which have been made by the other sex; naturally, this is so. Yet it is the masculine values that prevail. Speaking crudely, football and sport are 'important'; the worship of fashion, the buying of clothes 'trivial'. And these values are inevitably transferred from life to fiction. This is an important book, the critic assumes, because it deals with war. This is an insignificant book because it deals with the feelings of women in a drawing-room. A scene in a battlefield is more important than a scene in a shop – everywhere and much more subtly the difference of value persists.
>
> (*ROO*, 70–1)

'Naturally', each sex has its own values; yet once this is granted, it is not clear how or why the values 'made' by one come to take precedence over those of the other. The passage assumes a fundamental and natural difference between the sexes. It does not ask whether the distinction of 'important' from 'trivial', the inverted commas signalling a question as to their respective priority, is itself part of what 'the other sex' has made.

Given that there is a difference, but that one set of values succeeds in establishing a priority, it is only right, the passage implies, that the 'fair' sex should be given a hearing, and that women should come to be granted their different but equal place. Under the prevailing system, the nineteenth-century women writer was deflected from her natural values, 'pulled from the straight . . . in deference to external authority' (71): 'she was admitting that she was "only a woman", or protesting that she was "as good as a man"' (71). But again, Woolf's narrator singles out exceptions – Jane Austen and Emily Brontë: 'They wrote as women write, not as men write' (71).

The implied destination here is a situation where women will both catch up with men and cease to be deflected by them from their own path. There is a full and natural state, with its own set of values, proper to each sex. In themselves these values do not intrude upon or interfere with one another; each is the other's outside, and the 'impediment' that needs to be removed is the hierarchy that has established the one as superior to the other. In the meantime, women's writing can be identified as not yet women's writing, or as women's writing *manquée*, when it manifests the qualities of feminine self-abnegation ('"only a woman"') or masculine protestation ('"as good as a man"'), each of which comply with the dominant order by accepting that womanly values are less than men's.

Recovering a Female Tradition

> We think back through our mothers if we are women. It is useless to go to the great men writers for help, however much one may go to them for pleasure.
>
> (*ROO*, 72–3)

It is implicit in Woolf's assertion here that women writers need women writers as examples: if they are to write 'as women', they need to see that women have written (and not, for example, that men have written or simply that there has been writing). And Woolf has herself become foremother to a generation of feminists who 'think back through our mothers'. She pioneered the work of making known the writing of women whose existence had previously been obscured, covered over, by the weight of the masculine canon, and this enterprise has since become an industry on a large scale in both publishing and criticism. But demonstrating the existence of a body of women's writing, published and unpublished, is not the same as giving it a separate story: establishing it as an independent tradition with its own line of development. This is a different enterprise, which has also been widely undertaken and in many different ways.

Elaine Showalter's *A Literature of Their Own* (1979) traces such a development, her title alluding not only to Woolf's more singular *Room*, but also quoting from John Stuart Mill's speculations on a possible different style of women's literature in *On the Subjection of Women* (1869).[6] Showalter's is an evolutionary perspective, according to which women's separate and equally valid experiences and values are shown in their gradual emergence from under the suppression and distortion of patriarchal constraints. While Showalter criticizes Woolf in other ways, as will appear further on, she adopts a narrative model similar to the one implied by Woolf's own treatment of her not-yet-wholly-womanly literary mothers. Showalter's three phases of 'feminine', 'feminist' and (finally) 'female' writing correspond closely enough to Woolf's distinction between the early apologists ('only a woman'), the angry protesters ('as good as a man') and the women who at last succeed in getting their womanly values expressed on the page with 'integrity'.

Where the claim for 'a literature of their own' challenges the prevailing canon by showing it is not the only one, and showing it up as exclusively masculine, so the positing of a single and homogeneous female tradition has been challenged as equally imperialistic and exclusive. In a move that is structurally identical to that of the opening feminist challenge, others point out in turn the unacknowledged norms of race, class and sexuality (i.e. white, middle-class and heterosexual) implicit in what is now labelled 'mainstream' feminist criticism. At the same time, independent traditions belonging to the various marginalized groups are unearthed and provided with their own histories.[7]

Elsewhere, Woolf too draws attention to factors other than the writer's sex and the time of writing that bear upon different uses of language and different literary possibilities. In *A Room*, as we shall see, she underlines the difference of a novel about a lesbian relationship, and in a short piece introducing a volume of autobiographical writing by working-class women she stresses the differences between women of different social classes, both in the experiences that form them and in the kind of language which they use.[8]

Those who challenge the mainstream patriarchal 'canon' generally try to avoid setting up what only turns out to be another definitive list of the best and the greatest. In Woolf's discussion of what women's writing is, she usually draws on the names that are already known and already in print. For the nineteenth century, for instance, her examples are Eliot and the Brontës, the same women singled out habitually as having produced work worthy of a place in the 'common' canon or the 'great tradition' of English literature. In her programmatic statements, however, she suggests more that it is 'obscure' writing, the works of 'Anon' – who, she says, was probably most often a woman – that need to be brought to notice.[9]

On the other side of this, she also hints that some of the best-known women writers have been 'overdone':

> And, after all, we have lives enough of Jane Austen; it scarcely seems necessary to consider again the influence of the tragedies of Joanna Baillie upon the poetry of Edgar Allan Poe; as for myself, I should not mind if the homes and the haunts of Mary Russell Mitford were closed to the public for a century at least.
>
> (*ROO*, 45)

It is another uncanny anticipation of the destiny of the name 'Virginia Woolf': as part of the coffee-table book cult of 'Bloomsbury', as the object of a feminist cult of the 'great foremother'; and – to modify Mrs Ramsay's explanation of Charles Tansley's thesis topic (*TL*, 22) – as the object of numerous critical studies about 'the influence of something' upon her.

Another turn to the process of thinking back through our mothers is suggested by Woolf's fable of Shakespeare's hypothetical sister Judith, unable because of her sex to fulfil theatrical gifts equal to her brother's. The fictional reconstruction highlights the fact that it is impossible to know whether such a sister did or did not exist, since what it relates is nothing else than how she would have been prevented from doing anything worthy of historical 'note': 'Let me imagine, since facts are so hard to come by' (46). Women also think back, perhaps, through the very fact of having 'no tradition behind them' (72): think back through the *absence* of mothers.

Sentences

> The sentence that was current at the beginning of the nineteenth century ran something like this perhaps: 'The grandeur of their works was an argument with them, not to stop short, but to proceed. They could have no higher excitement or satisfaction than in the exercise of their art and endless generations of truth and beauty. Success prompted to exertion; and habit facilitates success.' That is a man's sentence: behind it one can see Johnson, Gibbon and the rest. It was a sentence that was unsuited for a woman's use.
>
> (*ROO*, 73)

The last two sentences of this passage are two of the most often quoted among Virginia Woolf's many thousands; the previous three, while described as one – 'That' – are identified as 'a man's', though written by the same woman. Many questions are broached here about the possibility of recognizing a difference of linguistic style according to the writer's sex, or that of determining the sex of the writer on the basis of stylistic evidence.

The passage proposes that there is a definite connection between sexual difference and language, but that its form is historically variable. Different sentences, it is implied, will be suitable for a man and a woman. Their identity as one or the other precedes the language they put to 'use' as a medium of expression, and the luck of historical accident decides whether or not the woman (or, by extension, the man) will find an appropriate sort of sentence available. One type of sentence only was 'current' at the beginning of the nineteenth century, and it was 'a man's'; a woman could write it (Woolf does so) but only, apparently, by taking up a man's materials or a man's identity: 'such a lack of tradition, such a scarcity and inadequacy of tools, must have told enormously upon the writing of women' (73).

But the seeming asymmetry between the grammatical situation of the two sexes deserves a closer look. 'A man's sentence' is at first sight possessive: the man with a sentence of his own, forged by himself and suitable for his use. The sentence belongs to him and not to the woman. She, by contrast, is passively placed in relation to the only available sentence (his), which is unsuited 'for' her use. This discrepancy between the genitive and the dative, between the sentence 'of' the man and the sentence 'for' the woman, indicates a differential access to the medium of language use: we are dealing with quite different cases, grammatically and judicially. Something about the man's sentence causes it to take precedence, to take control, while the woman's sentence simply does not exist, is nowhere 'current' or available for use.

But then it turns out that though there was no woman's sentence, some women might be exempt from the man's sentence: 'Jane Austen looked at it and laughed at it and devised a perfectly natural, shapely sentence proper for her own use and never departed from it.' (73). Here we return to the question of the exceptional writer, the exceptional woman. If Jane Austen is a woman and is capable of pronouncing her own sentence, that seems to throw doubt upon the general powerlessness attributed to women suffering from 'such a scarcity and inadequacy of tools' (73). What is the relation of what is 'proper' to the individual writer, woman or man, and what is general to their sex (or their class, or their race, or their historical provenance, for that matter)? What could it mean to 'devise' what is 'natural'? If 'a' Jane Austen, or indeed 'a' Virginia Woolf, can successfully fabricate a sentence suited to her use, then there must be some uncertainty as to the universality of the claim for the sexual division of sentences. The special case both disproves the rule and points to a different model of stylistic analysis. Man's sentence/woman's sentence divides the linguistic universe in two: a writer is one or the other, man or woman, and the sentence is adequate evidence as to the gender of its writer. Jane Austen's sentence/George Eliot's sentence (the latter 'committed atrocities with it that beggar description' (73)) suggests a degree of agency and idiosyncrasy denied by the initial model of women's forced compliance with a linguistic state of affairs which offers them no place. Read retrospectively, 'a man's sentence' might then seem to imply, as for the woman, the sentence available for the man, and the decisive distinction would in this case be not between the sexes, equally subject to the currency of suitable sentences, but between creative writers who make their own sentences, and the rest.

New Regions of Literature

> 'Chloe liked Olivia,' I read. And then it struck me how immense a change was there. Chloe liked Olivia perhaps for the first time in literature.
>
> (*ROO*, 78)

The hypothesis of a man's and a woman's sentence suggests that there is a difference in the form of the language suitable to each sex. Another of the models of gendered writing considered by Woolf's narrator focuses rather on the subject matter of women's fiction. Turning literature in the direction of women's values may produce quite new spaces and possibilities for fiction. The lectures which make up *A Room of One's Own* were delivered just before the trial of Radclyffe Hall's novel *The Well of Loneliness* (1928), which was prosecuted (and eventually suppressed) for its lesbian content. Though she privately regarded it as a 'meritorious dull book' (*D*, 3: 193), Woolf was willing to speak on its behalf. The pushing back of the frontiers of literary representation to open up new areas of women's experience was a cause worth defending.

In the passage above, Woolf claims that the novel of 'Mary Carmichael' is not just the first novel to treat of a lesbian relationship, but the first to allow the existence of friendship between women – their relations hitherto regarded, as with Cleopatra contemplating Octavia, with patriarchal eyes, as the jealous contention for men's favours. The expansion of the field of writing about women is thus at the same time bound to upset or transform the norms of masculine and feminine values. In regard to values, Woolf's example 'speaking crudely' was the different importance accorded to football and shopping (70). Just as she celebrates the extension of legitimate literary fields to the area of relationships between women, so she envisages the literary possibilities that might be offered by giving a place in literature to the 'feminine' shop:

> Mary Carmichael might well have a look at that in passing, I thought, for it is a sight that would lend itself to the pen as fittingly as any snowy peak or rocky gorge in the Andes. And there is the girl behind the counter too – I would as soon have her true history as the hundred and fiftieth life of Napoleon or seventieth study of Keats and his use of Miltonic inversion which old Professor Z and his like are now inditing.
>
> (*ROO*, 86)

The exploration of new literary countries is thus no neutral addition: it is also a challenge to the priority and interest of the mountain peaks of the present empire, preoccupied only with dramatic exploits and the lives of great men. While it is implied that the new fields of feminine literature are there to start with, only waiting for the pen to come along and borrow them, there is also the possibility that they might in some way be of a different, not just devalorized, order:

> For if Chloe likes Olivia and Mary Carmichael knows how to express it she will light a torch in that vast chamber where nobody has yet been. It is all half lights and profound shadows like those serpentine caves where one goes with a candle peering up and down, not knowing where one is stepping.
>
> (*ROO*, 80)

The hygienic and thoroughly well-lighted laboratory where the two women work has now been transformed into a much more mysterious space: a dark 'chamber', even a 'serpentine' cave. Is this buried region of unrepresented femininity enigmatic only until it is brought up into the bright lights of the modern novel? Is it a place, or a topic, like any other, only obscure until the torch is turned its way? Or is there something qualitatively different about it, something which will always give it this half-lit atmosphere of a place not so readily put on the general map?

The subterranean, shadowy imagery of this passage recalls the frequent allusions in one region of contemporary feminist theory to two of Freud's metaphors for femininity. In his essay on 'Female Sexuality' (1931), Freud compares the discovery of the significance of 'the early, pre-Oedipus, phase in girls' to that 'in another field, of the Minoan-Mycenaean civilization behind the civilization of Greece'. And in *The Question of Lay Analysis* (1926), he says: 'the sexual life of adult women is a "dark continent" for psychology'.[10] The conflation of historical and spatial obscurity in the archaeological analogy suggests that femininity in some way eludes or precedes the parameters of rationalistic representation; the '"dark continent"' suggests a vast expanse awaiting its enlightenment, but also the enigma of a space which cannot be assimilated to the norms of 'civilized' thought.

Exponents of what is called *écriture féminine*, notably Hélène Cixous, associate the 'dark continent' of femininity with both the unconscious and the body; feminine writing (which is not exclusively the province of women, since male artists are precisely those men who have not repressed the bisexual aspect of their own pre-Oedipal phase) is writing in which the body and the unconscious are expressed, are put into text, without the intervention of patriarchal codings and compartmentalizations ('Instantly a man's figure rose to intercept me . . .' (7)). In this view, feminine writing, by whichever sex, is writing which breaks up, or is somehow antecedent to, the conventions and boundaries of 'civilized' representation. It is not just one more new literary field, but that form of writing which throws into question the status of all the rest.

Writing the Body

> I want you to figure to yourselves a girl sitting with a pen in her hand, which for minutes, and indeed for hours, she never dips into the inkpot. The image that comes into my mind when I think of this girl is the image of a fisherman lying sunk in dreams on the verge of a deep lake with a rod held out over the water. She was letting her imagination sweep unchecked round every rock and cranny of the world that lies submerged in the depths of our unconscious being. Now came the experience that I

> believe to be far commoner with women writers than with men. The line raced through the girl's fingers. Her imagination had rushed away. It had sought the pools, the depths, the dark places where the largest fish slumber. And then there was a smash. There was an explosion. There was foam and confusion. The imagination had dashed itself against something hard. The girl was roused from her dream. . . . To speak without figure she had thought of something, something about the body, about the passions which it was unfitting for her as a woman to say. Men, her reason told her, would be shocked.
>
> ('Professions for Women', *CE*, II: 287–8)

Like the advocates of *écriture féminine*, Woolf also regarded the lack of representation of the body in literature as something which needed to be remedied; Jinny in *The Waves* declares ardently that 'My imagination is the body's' (*W*, 149). In the passage above, Woolf further implies that the body's present absence is an effect of suppression (of men as well as of women) on the part of men.

This passage closely parallels the mental angling episode near the beginning of *A Room*. The narrator has just settled down by the banks of the river to fish for her idea ('thought . . . had let its line down' (7)), when she is reprimanded, interrupted, by the Beadle. What the 'unchecked' imagination explores here has to do with both the body and the unconscious; it is figured as hidden in a submerged depth, like the buried civilization or the 'dark' continent; bringing it to the surface is shocking for men and provokes the rock-like resistance of 'something hard' in contrast to its own fluidity. Cixous uses a similar fishing image when she says: 'The truth, which lives only sheltered by silence, is forced to give evidence, and so it is in the same state as a fish pulled out of the water, thinking of the sea in a last convulsion, then, the end'.[11] It is as if the relational structure of language necessarily spells the end of the feminine 'truth', sentencing it to death. And this then raises a question as to the possibility of *écriture féminine* as such. For if it is defined as precisely that which cannot be represented, put into words, it must remain, like the woman's sentence, always elsewhere than in the 'current': always submerged in a region prior to or beyond that of language, from which it can only be brought into the light of representation at the price of assimilation and thus by the loss of what makes it different. *Écriture féminine* thus flounders somewhere between the invisibility of what lies hidden in the waves and the killing consistencies of the upper world. And this is perhaps why it is more difficult to catch the thing itself than to advocate or allude to it as that which cannot be fitted into the forms of language.[12]

Rewriting History

> It would be ambitious beyond my daring, I thought, looking about the shelves for books that were not there, to suggest to the students of those famous colleges that they should rewrite history, though I own that it often seems a little queer as it is, unreal, lop-sided; but why should they not add a supplement to history, calling it, of course, by some inconspicuous name so that women might figure there without impropriety? For one often catches a glimpse of them in the lives of the great, whisking away into the background, concealing, I sometimes think, a wink, a laugh, perhaps a tear.
>
> (*ROO*, 44–5)

At several points in the course of *A Room*, Woolf's narrator suggests lines for future research that her female student audience might like to pursue: an 'elaborate study of the psychology of women by a woman' (75); a study of the reasons for men's opposition to women's emancipation (54); research into the lives of ordinary women in different historical periods (44); 'the value that men set upon women's chastity' (61), for example. Like the extension of literature to accommodate women's writing about women, such projects will be more than mere addenda to the lines of volumes already existing in the British Museum and the university libraries: they will rewrite history in the sense indicated by the passage above, shifting the criteria for what is considered to count as relevant;

revealing as 'lop-sided' what was taken as straight and true; and challenging the standard histories of wars and campaigns which formerly stood in splendid isolation.

Other kinds of event will occupy the foreground, and it is significant that the one Woolf's narrator singles out in her adumbration of a rewritten history has to do with women and writing: 'Thus, towards the end of the eighteenth century a change came about which, if I were rewriting history, I should describe more fully and think of greater importance than the Crusades or the Wars of the Roses. The middle-class woman began to write' (62–3). Not only is fictional writing considered historically important, but 'rewriting' history now appears not so much as a rectification in the light of new evidence but as the telling of a different story, elicited by new questions asked of the evidence.

This suggests further a possible disturbance of conventional generic boundaries, a disturbance to which Woolf's own writing constantly aspires. In her essays she turns away from formal exposition to tell a story, and in her novels she attempts to shift the conventions that lay down the received distinctions of the factual and the poetical and the frequently correlated 'masculine' and 'feminine'. Woolf shied away from standard generic categories and experimented with new possibilities: *The Pargiters* was to be an 'Essay–Novel' (*D*, 4: 129), and *The Waves* 'a playpoem' (*D*, 3: 203). She even speculated on the possibility of abandoning such categories altogether: 'I have an idea that I will invent a new name for my books to supplant "novel". A new – by Virginia Woolf' (*D*, 3: 34).

The new writing of women is to have effects on both literature and history, equally subject hitherto to the dominance of the man's divisions. And the placing of both under one parasol may perhaps redress the balance of a monstrous division from which, Woolf stresses, it is women, not men, who have suffered: entirely ignored in the one, and blown up to excessive proportions in the other:

> A very queer, composite being thus emerges. Imaginatively she is of the highest importance; practically she is completely insignificant. She pervades poetry from cover to cover; she is all but absent from history. . . .

> It was certainly an odd monster that one made up by reading the historians first and the poets afterwards – a worm winged like an eagle; the spirit of beauty in a kitchen chopping up suet. But these monsters, however amusing to the imagination, have no existence in fact. What one must do to bring her to life was to think poetically and prosaically at one and the same moment. (*ROO*, 43)

The living woman is to be found in neither literature nor history; she might, however, be invented by some new combination of the two. That is not to say that she would be any more a creature of nature, since it is a new kind of writing which will bring her to 'life'.

Woolf's challenge to what she identifies as a masculine history (great wars, great nations, great men) anticipates the principles and practices of explicitly feminist history and the related development of the study of social history. If social history reveals the 'lop-sided' nature of what now appears as an old-fashioned, narrow focus on national history, feminist history in its turn has pointed out the specifically masculine tilt of such assumptions as to what is to constitute the hypothetical 'whole picture' of history. It makes a nice coincidence that the turn towards modern social history could be marked as having occurred 'in or about' the year of the publication of *A Room of One's Own*, with the founding of the French journal *Annales* in 1929.

New fields of research imply new premises, then, about what is to count as history. But Woolf's emphasis on the dichotomy between poetic and historical representations of women points also to a question of style. The first passage quoted above wryly suggests that the radical 'supplement' to history should slip in as if by the back door, using 'some inconspicuous name' to avoid an overt breach of decorum, and apparently maintaining the acceptable supporting roles of the women just glimpsed 'whisking away into the background' in the pages of 'the lives of the great'. The new history will make use of devices of indirection, simulating a perfect conformity to masculine prescriptions for proper feminine comportment while in the act of radically undermining them. The wink, the laugh and the tear of the women not quite hidden from history serve as models for strategies of feminist subversion – by mocking, upsetting and looking askance at the paternal proprieties and turning the practice of history-writing away from their appearance of sublime scholarly indifference and neutrality.

Margins and Mirrors

> Wherever one looked men thought about women and thought differently. It was impossible to make head or tail of it all, I decided, glancing with envy at the reader next door who was making the neatest abstracts, headed often with an A or a B or a C, while my own notebook rioted with the wildest scribble of contradictory jottings.
> (*ROO*, 30–1)

Women's exclusion from access to the means of being 'trained' (28) as a qualified scholar can also be read in a different way: as an openness to kinds of thinking ruled out by pedantic discipline. The stubborn insistence on reducing everything automatically to alphabetical order obscures the 'contradictory' matter which might otherwise become the basis of a less formulaic and less artificially consistent sequence of points.

'Woman', it seems, is the exemplary instance of what the trained masculine mind has to bring into line, to put in order. The 'woman' reader does not recognize herself in the assorted representations the books provide of this personage she abbreviates to 'W.'; and making a list, in an attempted imitation of her neighbour's methods, only brings her to a dead end: 'And if I could not grasp the truth about W. (as for brevity's sake I had come to call her) in the past, why bother about W. in the future?' (31). It is here, with the failure of the alphabetical procedure ('W' = ?), that the 'contradictory jottings' come into their own, and a lack of lists becomes the punning advantage of absent-mindedness:

> But while I pondered I had unconsciously, in my listlessness, in my desperation, been drawing a picture

> where I should, like my neighbour, have been writing a conclusion. . . . It was the face and the figure of Professor von X engaged in writing his monumental work entitled *The Mental, Moral, and Physical Inferiority of the Female Sex*. He was not in my picture a man attractive to women. . . . His expression suggested that he was labouring under some emotion that made him jab his pen on the paper as if he were killing some noxious insect as he wrote, but even when he killed it that did not satisfy him; he must go on killing it; and even so, some cause for anger and irritation remained.
>
> (*ROO*, 31)

The picture reveals to this 'W.' both her own anger at the man's representation of 'W.' and 'X''s own anger at 'W.': 'unconsciously' departing from the given terms of scholarly reference, her 'listlessness' results in a further question and reveals the professor's supposedly rational inventory to have been made in 'the red light of emotion' (33).

Doodling in the margins, against the main line of thought, proves to be a fruitful figure for the undirected speculations of Woolf's narrator. 'Drawing cart-wheels on the slips of paper provided by the British taxpayer for other purposes' (28) already hints at a mildly subversive activity; then 'my mind wandered' (28) in directions other than those of the man who knows where he is going:

> The student who has been trained in research at Oxbridge has no doubt some method of shepherding his question past all distractions till it runs into his answer as a sheep runs into its pen.
>
> (*ROO*, 28)

The 'trained' as opposed to the wandering, cartwheeling mind is here firmly snubbed, as reducing every question to fit its ready-made answer. And in the same gesture, the 'pen' – for Gilbert and Gubar the instrument and symbol *par excellence* of masculine literary authority – is punned into nothing more threatening than a tame retreat to which the sheep returns in blind obedience. The trained mind's pretensions are cut down to sheer conformity, with 'all distractions' holding far more interesting possibilities. Where he proceeds and processes along rigidly defined lines, the female narrator has the liberty, as well as the difficulty, of being without a fixed enclosure for writing – a pen of her own. And this contains the same ambivalence as the 'money and a room of her own' (6) declared as prerequisites for women to write: at once the necessity and the over-protection of a 'stable' situation, the source of an 'insider's' dumb security. Beadle or woman? Sheep or Woolf? The relative positions and identities become ever more difficult to sustain.

The jottings of 'W.' cast doubt on the plausibility and coherence of Professor X's lists, and suggest unsuspected interpretations for 'some of those psychological puzzles that one notes in the margin of daily life' (35). In particular, the revelation of the anger behind the professor's writing leads the narrator to a hypothesis about the structure of patriarchal thought:

> Women have served all these centuries as looking-glasses possessing the magic and delicious power of reflecting the figure of man at twice its natural size. Without that power probably the earth would still be swamp and jungle. . . . Mirrors are essential to all violent and heroic action. That is why Napoleon and Mussolini both insist so emphatically upon the inferiority of women, for if they were not inferior, they would cease to enlarge.
>
> (*ROO*, 35–6)

In a deft redrawing of conventional 'images' of the woman as narcissistic, Woolf here exposes a self-aggrandizing image of man as prior. Far from having any image of her own, or even functioning as an image for man to look at, women have only 'served' as the means of him seeing himself. But Woolf also suggests that such a looking-glass effect is perhaps essential: without it, 'the earth would still be swamp'. Implicitly, the solution would not be in a return to the 'natural' size, but in an alteration of the hierarchized sexual terms on which 'the looking-glass vision' presently rests. It is by means of the seemingly peripheral 'puzzles that one notes in the margin of daily life' that the ubiquitous mirroring function comes to be seen for what it is.

Luce Irigaray works with the same double identification of margins and mirrors in her analysis of texts from the tradition of western philosophy, beginning with Plato. In *Speculum: de l'autre femme*, she shows the complicity of intellectual and narcissistic ways of looking: men's discourse is forever seeking to represent, to 'speculate' upon 'woman', in his own image. She also practises a technique of 'marginal' writing, inserting her commentary literally between the lines of men's philosophical texts, including Freud's 1933 lecture on femininity.[13] Woolf suggests a similar strategy here. Just as *writing* includes a silent 'w', so 'W.' is endlessly represented, and misrepresented, in 'phallogocentric' writing, and so the woman reader can begin to break down the apparent coherence of that writing by questioning it on its own terms, by writing her own marginal comments, revealing the limits of logic there all the time but never before shown up.

At every point, *A Room of One's Own* insists on the possibilities of the 'wandering' over the 'trained' mind running on preconceived lines. This occurs partly by thematic hints: the opposition of the rigid austerity of the grounds of the men's college at Oxbridge and the 'wild, unkempt grasses' (20) of the women's. It is also effected through the structure of the lecture as a whole, which is cast in the form of a long digression – literally, a wandering off the main path – or indeed a 'pre-amble', describing the narrator's mental and physical strollings before she began to write. It is as if the topic of 'Women and Fiction', if it is not to consist in platitudes equivalent to those in the books of the British Museum, can only be approached indirectly, under the guise of merely leading up to it.

The strategy of marginal writing is not, however, to be taken as a licence for anarchy. The 'riot' of contradictory jottings is useful only if it turns out to switch back round to some further 'train of thought' (6, 104), or if it works as an implicit criticism of the masculine line to which it is juxtaposed. Woolf's narrator is firm in her reproof of the enthusiastic excesses of the Duchess of Newcastle, one of the early women writers she discusses: 'What a vision of loneliness and riot the thought of Margaret Cavendish brings to mind! as if some giant cucumber had spread itself over all the roses and carnations in the garden and choked them to death.' (59–60). Here, the 'riot' has gone too far, so out-naturing nature in its grotesque profusion as to be beyond any possible connection with, or criticism of, more cultivated lines of thought.

The Androgynous Mind

Of all the models of what constitutes the relation between 'women' and 'writing' in *A Room*, androgyny has provoked some of the wildest outbursts of indignation and celebration, and also some of the best-trained academic criticism. It thus seems worth quoting the principal offending or inspiring passage at some length.

> The sight of the two people getting into the taxi and the satisfaction it gave me made me also ask whether there are two sexes in the mind corresponding to the two sexes in the body, and whether they also require to be united in order to get complete satisfaction and happiness? And I went on amateurishly to sketch a plan of the soul so that in each of us two powers preside, one male, one female; and in the man's brain the man predominates over the woman, and in the woman's brain the woman predominates over the man. . . . If one is a man, still the woman part of his brain must have effect; and a woman also must have intercourse with the man in her. Coleridge perhaps meant this when he said that a great mind is androgynous. It is when this fusion takes place that the mind is fully fertilized and uses all its faculties. Perhaps a mind that is purely masculine cannot create, any more than a mind that is purely feminine, I thought.
>
> (*ROO*, 94)

'Man', 'woman', 'masculine' and 'feminine' are all known quantities or qualities, with each pair forming a complementary whole. The man and woman get into the taxi together, the masculine and feminine (or male and female) parts of the mind (of the woman or the man) are fused together. There is no apparent hierarchical order between them: the only dominance is of the feminine part in the woman's brain, and vice versa for the man. We are thus not dealing with anything like the hypothesis according to which 'W.' is a contradictory figment of the patriarchal imagination. Nor are we dealing with the hypothesis which says that men and women are entirely different animals, each with the right and the capacity for their own form of maturation and autonomy (though what androgyny has in common with this model is an endorsement of harmony and unity as the ideal state of the mind and of writing). Nor is this a historical hypothesis, indicating differing conditions for the social production of masculinity and femininity in various kinds of body. The two terms in each pair are offered without qualification, and as invariables.

Advocates of androgyny have found in the theory a model for a harmonious personality, wholesomely balancing two eternal sides of the human psyche usually stuck apart in different bodies. Nancy Topping Bazin, for instance, begins her book on *Virginia Woolf and the Androgynous Vision* as follows:

> Virginia Woolf would have agreed with D. H. Lawrence that human beings have two ways of knowing, 'knowing in terms of apartness, which is mental, rational, scientific, and knowing in terms of togetherness, which is religious and poetic.' Virginia Woolf associated these two ways with the two sexes.[14]

The passage first of all raises the question of whether, given these definitions of masculinity and femininity, androgyny is not inconceivable. For the fusion of the 'two ways of knowing' would itself have to be considered as an example of feminine 'togetherness'. Masculinity as 'apartness', would necessarily lose its separate identity in being brought together with femininity as 'togetherness'.

There is also a circularity to the argument: having stated what features are associated with each sex, it is a simple matter for Bazin to designate as androgynous those characters in the novels who are biologically of one sex but manifest features of the other. In the Woolf passage, bodily sex does indeed seem to determine the predominance of one or other mental sex, even though the traits to be associated with 'manly' and 'womanly' are not specified. Mental qualities are therefore less flexible than they may look at first sight: to say that male minds can be 'feminine' only reinforces the dualism according to which the difference between the two sexes is known in advance.

Ironically, then, one of the implications of this model of androgyny might be a reinforcement rather than an undoing of the habitual separation of sexual characters. But it has also come in for criticism from another angle: as seeming to reject the specificity of female subjectivity, effacing a difference which should rather be emphasized and valorized. Woolf's narrator later states categorically that 'it is fatal for anyone who writes to think of their sex' (99). That creative writers, of all people, should be singled out as those for whom their sex should not figure seems to constitute a denial of the necessity of asserting women's difference, whether psychological or in terms of their access to forms of literary expression. This is Elaine Showalter's principal objection to what she calls Woolf's 'flight into androgyny'; and Showalter also criticizes the erotic imagery of this passage which occurs further on:

> Some marriage of opposites has to be consummated. The whole of the mind must lie wide open if we are to get the sense that the writer is communicating his experience with perfect fullness. . . . Not a wheel must grate, not a light glimmer. The curtains must be close drawn. The writer, I thought, once his experience is over, must lie back and let his mind celebrate its nuptials in darkness. He must not look or question what is being done.
>
> (*ROO*, 99)

For Showalter, the slip at this point is to have made the writer not only explicitly male, but 'a male voyeur'.[15] But in fact the triangular structure here, as with the scene of the writer's spying on the couple getting into the taxi, can be taken to complicate the presentation of androgyny. The harmonious 'man-womanly' couple, in the street, in the room, in the writer's mind, is put at the distance of a satisfying scene for the narrator looking on. It is thus not simply represented as completeness, but set in the form of a *fantasy* of completeness and complementarity – between the sexes, within the mind, in the work of literature. The apparently simple duality of masculine and feminine is disrupted in this superimposition of the third element, the spectator.

The writer seems in fact to be placed in two different, equally ambiguous positions. In the first passage, s/he is a voyeur, actively looking and in control, seeing but unseen by the objects of his or her gaze. In the second passage, s/he is passive ('lie back and let his mind . . .'), as not understanding something that is going on elsewhere. In view of the sexual charge of the scenes, this seems to resemble the situation of the ignorant child, secretly witnessing or imagining what is not yet understood ('he must not look or question'). The first passage, on the other hand, like a film with a happy ending, suggests the adult's need for reassurance that all is well and normal out there, that nothing need threaten the wish to believe in the naturalness of a comfortable complementarity of masculine and feminine.

Both these positions suggested in the presentation of androgyny can be seen to figure in the explorations of sexual relations in Virginia Woolf's work; they transfer the issues of androgyny away from the hypothesis of gendered personality traits onto a terrain which is more concerned with the implied sexual structure of looking, and its relation to the practice of writing – 'as a woman', or indeed 'as a man'.

Showalter's pointing out that the 'darkened chamber' passage implies a male voyeur highlights a question about the significance of women writing that has been implicit in this discussion of Woolf's many approaches to the issue. Is the identification of writing as a male activity (the man's sentence, the male professional) to be taken as only a contingent, social restriction ('the sentence that was current at the beginning of the nineteenth century', for instance), or is there a more profound structure of enclosure and exclusion which makes of writing a practice which implies taking up a position identified as masculine?

When Woolf's narrator announces categorically that 'it is fatal for anyone who writes to think of their sex', there is something excessive about the forcefulness, and the threat, of the assertion. It occurs in a passage towards the end of *A Room* which is heavily underlined as representing the approach to a definite conclusion:

> Even so, the very first sentence that I would write here, I said, crossing over to the writing-table and taking up the page headed Women and Fiction, is that it is fatal for anyone who writes to think of their sex. It is fatal to be a man or woman pure and simple; one must be woman-manly or man-womanly. It is fatal for a woman to lay the least stress on any grievance; to plead even with justice any cause; in any way to speak consciously as a woman. And fatal is no figure of speech; for anything written with that conscious bias is doomed to death. It ceases to be fertilized.
>
> (*ROO*, 99)

It seems here that the man-woman is protesting too much the dangers of protestation: there is a grievance in the denunciation of grievance and a programmatic insistence in the censuring of 'any cause' as being unsuited to writing. After a hundred pages of meandering exploration of the different ways of thinking about the relationship of women and fiction, suddenly some force of censorship rises up like the Beadle himself to intercept such freedom, to sentence to death, a priori ('the very first sentence'), all the possibilities that the preamble has opened up.

There is also a curious slippage between the first and second parts of the passage. Initially, it is 'fatal for anyone', man or woman presumably, to think of his or her sex; then, it is 'fatal for a woman' to plead her case. This seems to precribe asymmetrical rules for the two sexes, and to leave the adjudication of such matters entirely in male hands, in the time-honoured manner. This would leave Mrs Brown, for instance, back where she started and without the right of 'protesting that she was different, quite different from what they made out' (*CE*, I: 333). By claiming that men and women should act indifferently with respect to writing, Woolf's narrator rules out the possibility that language may already be differentiating between them, and offers no means whereby a woman could utter her difference as a woman.

(And this may indeed be precisely the problem which it would be 'fatal' for the woman writer to acknowledge.) Ironically, then, the passage reinforces the existing differences in the very act of asserting their irrelevance.

The discrepancy noted here is paralleled in the first passage quoted on the androgynous writers: 'If one is a man, still the woman part of his brain must have effect; and a woman also must have intercourse with the man in her' (*ROO*, 94). For the man, there is only a 'woman part' of his brain, whereas the woman has 'the man' entire in her. This again would seem to suggest that the man-womanly combination in the ideal writer is not a union of two separate, equal and qualitatively different elements. Rather, the masculine dominates as whole to part, and we have returned to another version of the patriarchal structure.

Angel, Mother, Baby, Book

> Moreover, I thought, looking at the four famous names, what had George Eliot in common with Emily Brontë? Did not Charlotte Brontë fail entirely to understand Jane Austen? Save for the possibly relevant fact that not one of them had a child, four more incongruous characters could not have met together in a room . . .
>
> (*ROO*, 63–4)

Woolf's narrator hints at some relation between women's writing and childlessness. Considered socially, this might mean the incompatibility of the two activities, one consuming the time and emotional investment that would otherwise be used for the other. But there is also the possibility of a more complex symbolic connection. Traditionally, men's writing is represented as creation, on the analogy of childbearing; and in one version of this myth, the book is not just the equivalent but the substitute for the baby the man cannot literally produce. 'Natural' reproduction is thus taken as primary and enviable: the man seeks to make in another sphere what the woman is able spontaneously to produce in hers. In Woolf's case, the same analogy of writing and childbearing (or nurturing) figures, often enough, but with resonances that reveal a somewhat different symbolic structure.

In *A Room*, as we have seen, Woolf emphasizes that 'we think back through our mothers, if we are women'. These are metaphorical mothers, or mothers of metaphorical invention. What happens to a different mother figure of the would-be woman writer is quite the opposite. In 'Professions for Women', Woolf deals summarily with a character she identifies as 'the Angel in the House':

> You who come of a younger and happier generation may not have heard of her ... She was intensely sympathetic. She was immensely charming. She was utterly unselfish. . . . She sacrificed herself daily. . . . And when I came to write I encountered her with the very first words. . . . Directly, that is to say, I took my pen in my hand to review that novel by a famous man, she slipped behind me and whispered: 'My dear, you are a young woman. You are writing about a book that has been written by a man. Be sympathetic; be tender; flatter; deceive; use all the arts and wiles of our sex. Never let anybody guess that you have a mind of your own. Above all, be pure.' And she made as if to guide my pen. I now record the one act for which I take some credit to myself . . . I turned upon her and caught her by the throat. I did my best to kill her. My excuse, if I were to be had up in a court of law, would be that I acted in self-defence. Had I not killed her she would have killed me.
>
> (*CE*, II: 285–6)

The 'Angel' is quite explicitly a fictional rather than a real person: the phrase comes from the title of Coventry Patmore's bestselling nineteenth-century poem, so what is being represented here is the woman writer's need to do away with the standard images of femininity current in men's literature:

> She died hard. Her fictitious nature was of great assistance to her. It is far harder to kill a phantom than reality. ... But it was a real experience. It was an experience that was found to befall all women writers at

> that time. Killing the Angel in the House was part of the occupation of the woman writer.
>
> (*CE*, II: 286)

But the reference to the potency of a distorted, man-made figure of femininity is placed rather differently from the demand for a fairer treatment for Mrs Brown. Here, the literary representation of woman proves to be an inhibition to the prospective woman writer: changing the current appearance of the sex is not some routine task no sooner seen than done, but rather involves the removal of what is understood to be a ban. And here the agent of that censorship is not 'the figure of a man', but the Angel herself, whose fictional, phantom-like status proves to be all the more insidious.

The 'real experience' of killing the fictitious angel archly makes manifest the difficulty of treating matters of sexual identification with the supposed objectivity and neutrality of the court of law where the woman writer hypothetically offers her defence. And this 'real experience' reveals another side to the notion that we 'think back through our mothers', one which involves not the assumption but the putting away of a femininity taken to be not only incompatible with but actively censorious of a woman writing. Woolf's 'Angel' explicitly identifies writing as an unwomanly manner of behaving; her own sacrificial femininity is itself over-represented in Woolf's parody in order to render the murder all the more justifiable.

By the end – if it is an end – of *A Room*, Virginia Woolf, like Mary Carmichael, has indeed broken every conceivable norm or sentence and sequence, in questioning from a multiplicity of angles the possible and impossible answers to the problems found to be lurking behind her topic. The next chapters will consider three of Woolf's novelistic ventures into analysing the 'conditions' of masculinity and femininity. In *Orlando*, she shows that there is no logical base to received ideas of these conditions, while in *To the Lighthouse* and *Mrs Dalloway*, she looks at what they imply in the present organization of sexual difference. *To the Lighthouse* becomes in part a woman's investigation of the question 'What does a man want?', and *Mrs Dalloway* an exploration of what a woman might become.

3 Orlando's Vacillation

Orlando's change of sex can be read in many different ways. Orlando starts off as the male heir to a grand country house from which forty counties can be surveyed; by the end, the country house is open to the public, and Orlando is a woman. If we were looking for an allegorical reading, the biography could well seem to trace a paradigmatic move from men's to women's values, exemplified in *A Room* as the difference between football and shopping (*ROO*, 70). And indeed, in the opening scene, Orlando is to be seen 'slicing at the head of a Moor which . . . was the colour of an old football' (*O*, 9); by the end, she is spending her time in department stores. The move from a man to a woman might imply a move away from the centuries of patriarchy, and the coming of a 'women's time' whose beginnings are symbolically marked somewhere in the eighteenth century. Or, it could be said to indicate a general 'feminization' of humanity. From active control, the typical human subject has declined, or adjusted, to a state of relative passivity: in place of the clear, controlling view from the top, s/he is a passenger on a lift in a store, carried involuntarily upwards, and randomly glimpsing arrays of merchandise when the door opens on each floor (187).[1]

The difference between these two allegorical readings recalls the problem of establishing meanings for 'male', 'female', 'masculine', 'feminine'. In the first view, the 'man' is identified with the 'ruling lines' (*JR*, 38) of power, and the new time of the 'woman' is what challenges this order. In the second view, 'feminization' is a metaphor for the abandonment (voluntary or imposed) of an identity regarded as strong and autonomous: the modern subject is feminine in so far as s/he is more open, or more susceptible, less able or seeking to exercise 'masculine' control. But though this subject is interchangeably male or female, in a biological sense, it does not alter the fact that the meanings of 'masculine' and 'feminine' are presupposed as, roughly, 'active' and 'passive'.

If I suggest that the answer can certainly be both of these, that is only perhaps to emphasize the form of the question which is indicated in the very name of Orlando and the title of her book: or/and (and/or) and/or.[2] For the answer to the question about the historical model is inseparable from the reading of Orlando's double sex. Is this extraordinary 'biography' a fantasy of the effacement, the whimsical ruling out, of a sexual differentiation which must, in reality, mark the forms of human subjectivity? And/or, is it a manifesto for a new world in which the difference of the sexes is no longer the principal determinant of the lines along which human subjects make their way? It might be that the very possibility of putting the question in the form of the 'and/or', without demanding a definite, single answer, is already 'feminine', in the sense of preceding or challenging the confidence of an unequivocal judgement.

In his lecture on 'Femininity', Freud writes: 'When you meet a human being, the first distinction you make is "male or female?" and you are accustomed to make the distinction with unhesitating certainty'.[3] It is precisely this obviousness of 'unhesitating certainty' which *Orlando* withholds from the outset.[4] The very first words introduce a gendered pronoun whose readability is immediately put in question: '"He" – for there could be no doubt of his sex, though the fashion of the time did something to disguise it' (*O*, 9). If it is true that the first distinction 'we' make on meeting someone is 'male or female?', then *Orlando*'s beginning exposes that quite openly: the denial of a doubt introduces a doubt, and the 'he' which serves as that initial classification, putting the person into one group or the other, is not allowed to stand without qualification. The hesitation demonstrates how this most basic of differences is at once linguistic and visual: the perception and the classification into one of two types normally go together without a pause, so that the difference between the two, the movement by which the sight is interpreted as evidence of one or the other sex, is never itself looked into. The opening of *Orlando* troubles, then, that most basic of paradigms according to which 'we' make sense of other people. In the same way, the mysteriousness of the royal personage presumably concealed inside the imposing vehicle that passes through London in *Mrs Dalloway* is solemnly established by the impersonal dictum that 'even the sex was now in dispute' (*MD*, 16). If it is not even clear whether Orlando is he or she, then it will not be possible to proceed with the story: the narrator is deprived of the basic linguistic certainties for establishing the status of a human subject.

The problem of knowing what sex Orlando is or has derives, we are to understand, from the 'fashion' which 'did something to disguise it'. This implies that it is indeed bodily features, visually ascertainable with the removal of any distracting 'disguise', which settle the question of a person's sex. But it would follow from this that the putting on of deceptive clothes (in Orlando's case, the fashion only does 'something', not enough, to disguise his maleness), might perhaps be sufficient to change the sex in the eyes of the beholder. And would that then settle the issue, and if so which way?

The relation of the outward appearance to the 'true' sex is elaborated later on in *Orlando*, after the change of sex has taken place or taken shape. The narrator presents two alternative views, in discussing the relation of Orlando's change of clothes to her change of sex:

> There is much to support the view that it is clothes that wear us and not we them; we may make them take the mould of arm or breast, but they mould our hearts, our brains, our tongues to their liking. So, having now worn skirts for a considerable time, a certain change was visible in Orlando . . . If we compare the picture of Orlando as a man with that of Orlando as a woman we shall see that though both are undoubtedly one and the same person, there are certain changes. The man has his

> hand free to seize his sword, the woman must use hers to keep the satins from slipping from her shoulders. The man looks the world full in the face, as if it were made for his uses and fashioned to his liking. The woman takes a sidelong glance at it, full of subtlety, even of suspicion. Had they both worn the same clothes, it is possible that their outlook might have been the same.
>
> (*O*, 117)

The clothes determine the potential for acting the part of either sex. The man is that which needs a free hand for a sword, the woman that which must preserve her modesty, lest too much of her body be seen: the female Orlando has already noted a causal connection between the exposure of her legs and the imbalance of a sailor perched on a masthead.[5]

The moulding of clothes, then, determines the way that the person looks at the world: the narrator here defines the difference between the pictures of Orlando before and after as between the straight look 'full in the face' and the 'sidelong glance'. The man regards 'the world' as his equal, a person like himself – whom he meets and recognizes and to which he accommodates himself 'as if it were made for his uses and fashioned to his liking'. There is a perfect circle here, a perfect fit between the fashioning of world and man as brothers in arms, with the man who looks retaining the upper hand (his sword at the ready) in relation to the world he seems to have made 'for his uses'. The language is similar to that of *A Room of One's Own* on the difference betwen male and female sentences (*ROO*, 73): whereas the 'man's sentence' seems to be his property, and ready-made for his possessive purposes, no such sentence is available for the woman to use. The man gets his customized linguistic clothing off-the-peg, while the woman is placed outside the world of fraternal fittings.

This then leads on to the situation of the woman whose attire furnishes her with another kind of 'outlook'. Her clothes are in need of perpetual adjustment, as if they are always about to reveal what she is always engaged in concealing. The ankle, for example, unwittingly exposed to the sailor poised on the masthead, immediately topples him from his position in commanding the view. But the 'sidelong glance' of the woman shows her place outside the magic circle, liable to, and/or capable of, looking with 'suspicion' or 'subtlety' at the world which the man regards with complete acceptance. Just as her failure to preserve the outward forms of clothing decorum would threaten the security of the man's world-view, so it is from her position of not fitting in – of constantly adjusting her attire, and of not being at one with the world – that the woman's 'sidelong glance' at the masculine world proceeds.

The narrator's second 'view' of the relation between the clothes and the sex is formulated as follows:

> That is the view of some philosophers and wise ones, but on the whole, we incline to another. The difference betwen the sexes is, happily, one of great profundity. Clothes are but a symbol of something hid deep beneath. It was a change in Orlando herself that dictated her choice of a woman's dress and of a woman's sex.
>
> (*O*, 117–18)

Ostensibly – on the surface, at a first glance – this second view states that the sexes are more than superficially distinguished. It is not that clothes make what is then perceived as an underlying difference, but that there really is an underlying difference, of which the clothes are but a 'symbol'. So the difference in Orlando was not an outward contingency – the fact that becoming female changed the kinds of clothes she was socially expected to wear – but 'a change in Orlando herself': the biological sex has compelling psychic accompaniments which will 'dictate' the 'choice' of clothes. But the passage continues a little differently:

> And perhaps in this she was only expressing rather more openly than usual – openness indeed was the soul of her nature – something that happens to most people without being thus plainly expressed. For here again, we come to a dilemma. Different though the sexes are, they intermix. In every human being a vacillation from one sex to the other takes place, and often it is only the clothes that keep the male or female likeness, while

> underneath the sex is the very opposite of what it is above.
>
> (*O*, 118)[6]

Orlando's predicament is generalized as a common condition of 'vacillation' between one sex and the other. But though we are here being given the view according to which clothes speak the (already existing) sex, rather than moulding it, it is only apparently in rare cases of 'openness' that the sex of the clothes will express the changed sex. Women's clothes could be expressing a woman or disguising a man. So even though clothes are clearly readable as representing (or 'expressing') one of two sexes, and even though 'underneath' there is, unequivocally, one sex or the other, they are effectively useless as evidence of which sex it is, since there is no way of knowing whether the wearer is wearing 'plainly' and openly or not.

There is also the question as to whether the sexes 'intermix' at one time (as would be implied by the androgyny model of *A Room*), or alternate over a period of the life of 'a human being'. This would be implied by the case of Orlando under review, but is then complicated by the difficulty of deciding what would determine the ongoing 'male or female likeness' to which the clothes still correspond. It is as though the narrator is here using the analogy, or the image, of physical difference (what's 'underneath' the clothes as conclusive evidence) to talk about a psychic form of sexual identity which is actually something quite different. But then, to follow the same clothing image, if there is no necessary correspondence between the psychological and the biological sex, the travesty of the biological would be installed right from the beginning of the identification with one gender or the other. Even if it could be established whether the clothes did or did not correspond to the sex beneath, there would be a further layer to unpeel in deciding whether that sex too concealed a different one. Far from establishing a stable correspondence of clothes to underlying sex, this second view offers rather a potentially endless series of layers through which the sex is not just contingently but necessarily 'in dispute'.

There has been a considerable move away, then, from the ostensible model of this second description. If clothes ideally express the underlying sex, they may also be a secret, a cover, that conceals it, and the viewer has no means of telling which is which. The clothes offer an image which resembles that of a man or a woman; a woman's clothes may either express a woman, or hide a man; a 'woman' may be only the temporary appearance or inclination of a 'human being' who vacillates from one identity to the other – and vice versa in both cases. The surface/reality structure of the argument leaves no ground at all for choosing a perspective from which to judge accurately. There are always two levels; either the surface mirrors, or it travesties, the underlying reality. And there are therefore always, potentially, two sexes (at one time, rather than at different times), the one on the surface and the one underneath.

Looking at the narrator's two views as to the relation of clothes and sexual identity, their own alleged difference seems, as a result, to disappear. If the sex 'underneath' does not provide a firm point of reference for the second model, then the clothes return, as in the first model, as the only evidence to go on. There is an 'and/or' concealed behind the definite premises of both hypotheses, which turn out to be mutually implicated in such a way as to render undecidable, if not to obliterate, the distinction between them, which becomes itself another 'and/or'.

But the peculiar combinations and differences of view here also evoke the 'sidelong' or suspicious way of looking attributed in the first option to women. One of the 'ands' connecting, rather than differentiating, the first and the second model may be the uncertain, questioning look of the woman 'outside', and the 'vacillation' attributed to every human being. It is as though the indeterminacy of sexual difference is only acknowledged, or even broached, from a feminine position. These narrative speculations are only engendered, after all, by Orlando's change of sex in the direction of femininity, and the narrator's subsequent attempt to come to terms with it.

Orlando is full of characters whose sex turns out to be other than it seemed at first glance. There is the Archduke who falls for Orlando as a man, and so disguises himself as a woman to gain the opportunity to further his suit, dropping the deception when Orlando turns into a woman ('A heap of clothes lay in the fender. She was alone with a man' (111)). There is Sasha, first love of the young male Orlando, whose indeterminacy makes her all the more interesting: 'He beheld . . . a figure which, whether boy's or woman's, for the loose tunic and trousers of the Russian fashion served to disguise the sex, filled him with the highest curiosity' (23). There is the reversed identification between Orlando and her nineteenth-century husband, 'Marmaduke Bonthrop Shelmerdine, Esquire':

> An awful suspicion rushed into both their minds simultaneously.
>
> 'You're a woman, Shel!' she cried.
>
> 'You're a man, Orlando!' he cried.
>
> Never was there such a scene of protestation and demonstration as then took place since the world began.
>
> (*O*, 157)

There is the encounter of the female Orlando, dressed as a man, with Nell, the London prostitute with whom she establishes a close rapport having once 'flung off all disguise and admitted herself a woman' (135–6).

But this last example suggests something more about the relation of vacillation to the sex 'underneath'. The narrator states just after this that Orlando 'found it convenient at this time to change frequently from one set of clothes to another' (137), a mobility of sexual identity in which she did not engage as a man. The fact that she finds it 'convenient' indicates that her flexibility is a free choice: though she is a woman, she can choose to look like a man. This is like the first description of the relations between clothes and sex in so far as the clothes then make Orlando, to all intents and purposes, a man once more until she puts off her 'disguise'.

What Orlando adopts, then, is a strategy whereby as a woman she will have the best of both sexual worlds, posing at whim as one sex or the other, the difference being produced by a change of clothes. This 'vacillation' confounds the security of the structure in which the two sexes can be confidently distinguished, by reducing its determinants to a matter of outward appearances, simulating what may or may not be the true identity 'underneath'. But the deliberate choice of the masculine appearance implies that for a woman, the masculine identity is desirable (in this case, it opens more doors to her, taking her inside Nell's room): she has, as it were, a vested interest in being able to change from one sex to the other.

But this capacity for vacillation is itself what marks her femininity in the eyes of the biographer professing a concern to establish the true facts of her behaviour:

> As we peer and grope in the ill-lit, ill-paved, ill-ventilated courtyards that lay about Gerrard Street and Drury Lane at the time, we seem now to catch sight of her and then again to lose it. The task is made still more difficult by the fact that she found it convenient at this time to change frequently from one set of clothes to another.
> (*O*, 137)

The biographer is concerned to establish evidence with regard to the person he has already identified as female, peering with interest at her multifarious appearances.

But is he a 'he'? In the previous paragraph, the narrator has indeed been at pains to establish his own identity with respect to possible sexes. This follows immediately after the exchange of womanly confidences between Orlando and Nell and her friends:

> Many were the fine tales they told and many the amusing observations they made, for it cannot be denied that when women get together – but hist – they are always careful to see that the doors are shut and that not a word of it gets into print. All they desire is – but hist again – is that not a man's step on the stair? All they desire, we were about to say, when the gentleman took the very words out of our mouths. Women have no desires, says this gentleman, coming into Nell's parlour; only affectations. . . . Since . . . it is well known (Mr T.R. has proved it) 'that women are incapable of any feeling of affection for their own sex and hold each other in the greatest aversion', what can we suppose that women do when they seek out each other's society?

> As that is not a question that can engage the attention of a sensible man, let us, who enjoy the immunity of all biographers and historians from any sex whatever, pass it over, and merely state that Orlando professed great enjoyment in the society of her own sex, and leave it to the gentlemen to prove, as they are very fond of doing, that this is impossible.
>
> (*O*, 136–7)

Until the declaration of 'immunity' from sex, the narrator appears to be a woman: she has witnessed what goes on in the women's room from which men are excluded, and from which she reacts to the interruption of the 'man's step' threatening to break up the party of 'women together'; she is about to inform her readers of women's desires, against the prevailing gentlemanly consensus that they have none. But then of what sex are the implied readers who need to be enlightened on this matter? And does not the third person pronoun (what 'they' desire) put women at a certain distance already from the narrator? If something other than a man, 'she' is also less, or more, than a woman.

With her/his protestation of neutrality, the biographer then appears to be in a position not unlike that of Orlando. But if Orlando, in this case, is a woman posing as a man and thereby gaining a double vantage point, the biographer might well be a man posing as a woman, his alleged neutrality gaining him entry into the women's secret quarters so that he can deliver an authentic insider scoop to the outside world, with the authority of one whose insistent peering and groping into the feminine object of his study will finally settle the truth of her identity in no uncertain terms. The fact that this whole passage is heavily ironic further complicates the problem. The neutrality of biographers and historians is parodied as only an impossible pose (covering a certain sex underneath, presumably), and if the dismissal by the conventionally 'sensible man' of women's desires as non-existent is implicitly changed into an active interest in them ('engage the attention'), we are still left with a narrator who has a sex but is something other than a woman writing to or for women.

This might suggest some further speculations. *Orlando* tells the story of how a young man becomes a woman; but how, as a woman, she is forever vacillating between the sexes, as if femininity is an inherently unstable position, or as if its very condition is that of putting on and off the identities of one or the other sex. Orlando's biographer puts her/himself in an observer's position in regard to her. He is out to establish the facts – of her true nature, her true sexual identity. She is the one who is always changing (she either 'really' changes sex, or she pretends to, and it might be just a matter of narrative whim to determine which is which); he ('for there could be no doubt of his sex' (9) in this regard) is not in question, except in that he exposes the myth of his own (narrative and sexual) neutrality. But then that is the all-important qualification: it is as if *Orlando*'s biographer is only simulating, and exaggerating, the conventions expected of the would-be neutral biographer.

Part of a young gentleman's Cambridge education in *Jacob's Room* is to answer the question 'Does History consist of the Biographies of Great Men?' (*JR*, 36). *Orlando* unsettles every premise on which such a question might be based (among other things, the book must be the daughter's mockery of Leslie Stephen: Woolf's father was the editor of the first edition of the ultimate in the pedantic genre of representative 'lives', the *Dictionary of National Biography*). It is not so much that History might now consist of the Biographies of Great Women, but that it is not clear what a woman would be or who (man or woman or one 'immune' from sex) might be qualified to establish her identity one way or the other. *Orlando*'s playfulness masks a set of quite serious questions about the significance or determinability of sexual difference, as of the nature of history or of a coherent 'life'. And that very structure of one thing masquerading as another, or of 'playing' with different possibilities, might itself, in the terms of the novel, be the strategy of the feminine position outside the masculine circle of perfect harmony and consistency. The masculinity of the narrator might thus be another pose on which to cast a feminine 'sidelong glance'. But this hardly settles anything about the sex, or immunity from it, of the playfully serious pseudo-biographer.

It does, perhaps, shed a different light on the perspective of the androgynous writer in *A Room*. *Orlando*'s narrator ends up as something like a woman posing as a man posing as a woman to investigate the identity of a man who becomes a woman and poses as a man. It is as though every ground rule for establishing norms of biographical and historical narration goes out of the window, or 'falls from the masthead', once the sex is put in permanent dispute and permanent vacillation. In this novel, Woolf as masculine and feminine, footballer and shopper, allows herself a free kick or a free look at all the norms, taking to the limit the idea that they are reducible to a game or spectacle of masks and pretences, without any foundation to prop them up.

If this is a feminine strategy – unmasking the pretensions of masculine neutrality and playing up the possibilities of endless dissimulation of identity – it is anything but passive, and might indeed have something to add to the question of the difference between football and shopping. The masculine side is itself defined by the opposition of two opposed sides, and the object of scoring against the others; while feminine shopping is not antagonistic. Masculine football, further, plays absolutely according to rules that are fixed and regulate the position and functions of each player; whereas shopping involves experimentation and the possibility of putting on different clothes to make or conceal an infinitely mobile identity.

But this model of endless oscillation between one position, or one appearance, and another could itself be said to keep hidden other questions about what makes the difference of the sexes. The fact that Orlando becomes a mother almost incidentally, while her production of a literary masterpiece is the culmination of a labour of several centuries, might offer a clue that would take the analysis in a different direction.

Throughout Woolf's writing, artistic creation by women is figured as both a symbolic equivalent for mothering and something which is incompatible with actual mothering.[7] This suggests either – as with Miss La Trobe in *Between the Acts* – being placed in a masculine position (as the Angel says in 'Professions for Women', to write is unwomanly; by writing, a woman becomes like a man), and/or – as with Lily

Briscoe in *To the Lighthouse* – the not-yet-adult position of the child or daughter, looking on at the strange spectacle of 'man–womanly' relations.

Only in *Orlando*, as Françoise Defromont points out, do writing and motherhood go together; and there is something very peculiar about the difference in the accounts of how the two creations emerge.[8] Orlando's epic poem, 'The Oak Tree', lovingly gestated over hundreds of years, is erotically produced from her breast for the male critic's approval after being rushed into town for an emergency delivery:

> Orlando had not yet realized the invention of the steam engine, but such was her absorption in the sufferings of a being, who, though not herself, yet entirely depended on her, that she saw a railway train for the first time . . . without giving a thought to 'that stupendous invention . . .'
>
> (*O*, 171)

The actual baby, on the other hand, emerges almost parenthetically: in the formal style of a newspaper announcement, and from the hands of another woman rather than from Orlando's own body:

> 'It's a very fine boy, M'Lady', said Mrs Banting, the midwife, putting her first-born child into Orlando's arms. In other words Orlando was safely delivered of a son on Thursday, March the 20th, at three o'clock in the morning.
>
> (*O*, 185)

The relations between mothering, writing and the female body in these passages suggest a further direction of exploration: not this time in relation to the interchangeability in theory of masculine and feminine sexes, but to the actual dominance of the masculine and its construction of a femininity in or as its own image. If *Orlando* is at once a demonstration of the groundlessness of existing differences, and a fantasy that they might be simply discounted, *To the Lighthouse* looks at how the undeniably dominant masculine sets the terms for the possible identities of both men and women.

4 Getting to Q: Sexual Lines in *To the Lighthouse*

A train arrives at a station. A little boy and a little girl, brother and sister, are seated in a compartment face to face next to the window through which the buildings along the station platform can be seen passing as the train pulls to a stop. 'Look', says the brother, 'we're at Ladies!'; 'Idiot!' replies his sister, 'Can't you see we're at Gentlemen'.[1]

From this journey also dated the beginning of a 'phobia' of travelling by train, from which [Freud] suffered a good deal for about a dozen years (1887–99) before he was able to dispel it by analysis. It turned out to be connected with the fear of losing his home (and ultimately his mother's breast) – a panic of starvation which must have been in its turn a reaction to some infantile greed. Traces of it remained in later life in the form of slightly undue anxiety about catching trains.[2]

He was safe, he was restored to his privacy. He stopped to light his pipe, looked once at his wife and son in the window, and as one raises one's eyes from a page in an express train and sees a farm, a tree, a cluster of cottages as an illustration, a confirmation of something on the printed page to which one returns, fortified, and satisfied, so without his distinguishing either his son or his wife, the sight of them fortified him and satisfied him and consecrated his effort to arrive at a perfectly clear

> understanding of the problem which now engaged the energies of his splendid mind.
>
> (*TL*, 52–3)

This is Mr Ramsay securing sustenance from the image of his wife and son. The picture of familial harmony is analogous to the distant sight of the emblems of a pastoral idyll (farm, tree, 'cluster' of cottages), and the whole paragraph – a single sentence – is like an enactment in miniature of the structure of masculine subjectivity as Woolf analyses its impasses for both sexes in *To the Lighthouse*.

Mr Ramsay is (as if) on a train: he is moving at a fast rate along a line with a precise destination, and his 'effort' is 'to arrive' at a solution to his current 'problem'. In this endeavour, Mr Ramsay or the traveller is 'restored', 'fortified' and 'satisfied' – given strength, and given enough, like adequate nourishment – by seeing the image of rural completeness, and this is explicitly likened to the sight of the wife and child. In the same way, Mr Ramsay's 'problem' is validated in a quasi-religious sense – it is 'consecrated' – by the image of maternal wholeness. But the view from the train is also related to the text the passenger is reading. The far-off image gives 'confirmation' to what, it is implied, is the actual source of meaning on 'the printed page', but which is yet in some way lacking. It functions oddly both as secondary in relation to the meaning of the page, and as prior to the establishment of that meaning, 'to which one returns'.

This passage is immediately followed by another, much more famous one, which by picking up on the 'splendid mind' might seem to act in turn as its 'confirmation':

> It was a splendid mind. For if thought is like the keyboard of a piano, divided into so many notes, or like the alphabet is ranged in twenty-six letters all in order, then his splendid mind had no sort of difficulty in running over those letters one by one, firmly and accurately, until it had reached, say, the letter Q. He reached Q. Very few people in the whole of England ever reach Q. . . . But after Q? What comes next? After Q

> there are a number of letters the last of which is scarcely visible to mortal eyes, but glimmers red in the distance. Z is only reached by one man in a generation. Still, if he could reach R it would be something. . . . Q he could demonstrate. If Q then is Q – R –
>
> (*TL*, 53–4)

We might liken this, first of all, to the simile of the previous paragraph. If Mr Ramsay is still in some way (like) a train passenger, the rails along which he travels have now become the letters of the alphabet, which also lead to a preordained destination that 'glimmers red in the distance' like the lights of a station. It is as if the letters on the printed page have been transposed so as to fuse with the stages of the journey: 'getting from A to B', in this account, would be equivalent to getting from A to Z. But the effect of this is to render them less, not more, meaningful. Whereas the page, by implication, could be understood to have a meaning of which the far-off picture was then a 'confirmation' – both the page and the image working as heterogeneous signs of the same meaning – the letters of the alphabet have no meaning at all but are simply listed, by convention, in one particular order, with each one being defined in terms of its adjacency to two others (or one other, in the case of the first and the last).

The 'splendid mind' makes of the moves from A to B to C a logical rather than simply a linear progression, and so lays claim to more significance than the alphabetically ordered lists of the British Museum reader in *A Room of One's Own* (*ROO*, 30–1). 'If Q then is Q – R -' takes up the notation of propositional logic, and suggests that each letter attained is an advance upon the previous one, not just a neutral point on a line made up of points of equal value. Woolf is able to get maximum comic mileage out of the fact that P and Q really are the letters conventionally used as signs in propositional logic, while Mr Ramsay's name begins with the 'next' letter, R. (There is extra mileage too, perhaps, for a certain V.W. from the fact that her own consecutive initials are further along; and in that R is indeed often wheeled on in formal logic examples where a third letter is required in addition to P and Q . . .)

A further hint of an undermining of the main line of the simile occurs via the keyboard analogy, introduced at the beginning and then abandoned. For a keyboard's letters, though certainly sequential, go from A to G and then back to the beginning again: the bottom and top notes in terms of pitch may well have the 'same' name. And the move from the bottom to the top end of the keyboard – the piano being rather like the printed page with its implicit direction from left to right – involves repetitions rather than progression, when viewed in terms of letter names. The repercussions of this tacit conflation of the repetition and the sequence extend, as we shall see, to the differential and intersecting lines of each sex's 'normal' development.

In his *Three Essays on the Theory of Sexuality* (1905), Freud suggests a close connection between fantasies and trains: 'The shaking produced by driving in carriages and later by railway-travel exercises such a fascinating effect upon older children that every boy, at any rate, has at one time or other in his life wanted to be an engine driver or coachman.'[3] The fact that having first said that the fascination of trains affects 'older children' in general, Freud then signals this kind of dream as every boy's, is suggestive. Going back for a moment to Woolf's simile of the alphabet and piano ('If thought is like the keyboard . . .'), we might say: 'If masculine development is like a train journey . . .', and then see how far this takes us.

Woolf's explorations of what makes the difference of the sexes are uncannily close to Freud's in another key, and this may be related to the fact that his writings were much discussed in Woolf's social circle. The Hogarth Press, which she founded with her husband Leonard Woolf, published the first translations of Freud in Britain (and later, in the fifties and sixties, the Standard Edition).[4] Woolf drew directly on psychoanalytic insights in her prose writings (especially *Three Guineas*), but she also made use of them in her fiction. *To the Lighthouse* is particularly interesting in this regard because Woolf said of its writing: 'I suppose I did for myself what psycho-analysts do for their patients. I expressed some very long felt and deeply felt emotion. And in expressing it I explained it and then laid it to rest' (*MB*, 94). This declaration gives critics justification for the identification of

Woolf with Lily Briscoe, the daughter figure and artist as outsider who then looks back at the relation between her 'parents' and hers to them.

In the psychoanalytic account of human development, there is no subjectivity without sexual difference, and there is no natural, programmed progression for those of either biological sex towards the achievement of the 'masculine' or 'feminine' identity socially ascribed. Because the dominant line is that of masculinity, the girl's understanding of the meaning of sexual difference implies coming to terms with her *de facto* eccentricity, forced to take up a position in relation to the norm from which she is by definition excluded: as the image of maternal fulfilment seen from the train window, as the 'woman' despised for her lack of the masculine attribute, or as an interloper into the compartment reserved for men.

One way of looking at masculine development would be to say, in the teleology of social purpose, that its object is to get the boy onto the train, headed for a respectable destination, but still fired at some level by the fantasy of being Casey Jones at the throttle. But this is to go too fast, or to look only from one direction: put the other way around, the same process appears also as an inevitable lack of fit between the situation of the social subject as passenger and his residual fantasy of being, in the end, a hero. The mother figures in both perspectives as the imagined plenitude of a childhood left behind, but still there as the source of meaning and authentification for the work or journey in progress. Freud says that a man seeks in adult life to find again, in the form of a wife, the figure of support to whom he 'returns' for reassurance of his powers and centrality. Yet this reassurance refers to what he none the less lacks, to the extent that the social train admits him only at the price of a ticket which makes him like every other conforming passenger who has accepted the conditions of travel.

Mr Ramsay's blundering towards a possible R which will never be the Z of 'one man in a generation' perfectly illustrates such a pattern. He is likened to the resigned leader of an unsuccessful expedition:

> How many men in a thousand million, he asked himself, reach Z after all? Surely the leader of a forlorn hope may

> ask himself that . . . Mr Ramsay squared his shoulders and stood very upright by the urn.
>
> Who shall blame him, if, so standing for a moment, he dwells upon fame, upon search parties, upon cairns raised by grateful followers over his bones? Finally, who shall blame the leader of the doomed expedition, if, having adventured to the uttermost, and used his strength wholly to the last ounce and fallen asleep not much caring if he wakes or not, he now perceives by some pricking in his toes that he lives, and does not on the whole object to live, but requires sympathy, and whisky, and some one to tell the story of his suffering to at once? Who shall blame him? Who will not secretly rejoice when the hero puts his armour off, and halts by the window and gazes at his wife and son . . . and bending his magnificent head before her – who will blame him if he does homage to the beauty of the world?
>
> (*TL*, 55–7)

The 'expedition' – a journey with a goal, the attainment of which would ensure immortal fame to the leader – remains as the structuring fantasy for the philosopher resigned to getting no further than half-way, to being one of the 'plodding and persevering' rather than a man of 'genius': 'the gifted, the inspired who, miraculously, lump all the letters together in one flash' (55). And in the age of the train, the journey is figured in the more heroic imagery of the pioneering explorer.

Even Mr Ramsay's 'abstract' philosophical speculations seem to be related to the need to come to terms with a social hierarchy of men in which he does not necessarily occupy the place of 'genius':

> Does the progress of civilization depend upon great men? Is the lot of the average human being better now than in the time of the Pharoahs? Is the lot of the average human being, however, he asked himself, the criterion by which we judge the measure of civilization? Possibly not. Possibly the greatest good requires the

> existence of a slave class. The liftman in the Tube is an eternal necessity.
>
> (*TL*, 67)

Here the path of the individual is transposed to the field of 'civilization', which is also endowed with a hypothetical line of progression whose 'measure' can be decided. In this context of the great man *manqué*, it is the picture of maternal plenitude – his own wife and child, the reverenced 'beauty' of the woman – which provides, restores, a form of compensation. This is not incompatible with the fact that the acquisition of dependants in the form of wife and children – the settling down to the normality of the 'average' man – is also, in Mr Bankes's view, the reason for Mr Ramsay's failure to fulfil his early promise as a philosopher. The woman is placed in the contradictory position of being both source of meaning for the masculine project (that which 'fortifies' the traveller) and a constraint, the scapegoat for its necessary failure in the original heroic mode of its conception.

Mr Ramsay's relation to his wife suggests the man's wish to return to the position of the child in relation to a woman like his mother. According to Freud, it is in so far as she identifies with her mother that the woman:

> acquires her attractiveness to a man, whose Oedipus attachment to his mother it kindles into passion. How often it happens, however, that it is only his son who obtains what he himself aspired to! One gets an impression that a man's love and a woman's are a phase apart psychologically.[5]

The resentment of James – 'hating his father' (50) – for Mr Ramsey's prior claims to his mother parallels Freud's Oedipal scenario, where the boy wants nothing less than to put out of the way the father who asserts his rights to the mother. Looking at it from the husband's point of view, Mr Ramsay attempts to recover, with another woman, the relation of dependence and centrality in which he once stood, or imagines he once stood, to his own mother: after receiving the sympathy he claims from his wife, he is 'like a child who drops off satisfied' (60). Yet this harmony of oneness with the mother figure, which his wife is called upon to secure, can necessarily never be restored completely once it is posed in terms of a constitutive loss. Mr Ramsay's demands for reassurance of his uniqueness are doomed to be endlessly repeated: 'This was one of those moments when an enormous need urged him, without being conscious what it was, to approach any woman, to force them, he did not care how, his need was so great, to give him what he wanted: sympathy' (225). Only in fantasy can the exorbitant request be satisfactorily answered:

> Sitting in the boat, he bowed, he crouched himself, acting instantly his part – the part of a desolate man, widowed, bereft; and so called up before him in hosts people sympathising with him; staged for himself as he sat in the boat, a little drama; which required of him decrepitude and exhaustion and sorrow . . . and then there was given him in abundance women's sympathy, and he imagined how they would soothe him and sympathise with him.
>
> (*TL*, 247–8)

Other men in the novel are represented as threatened in similar ways in that identity, and seeking to have it given or restored to them through the intercession of an all-providing Mrs Ramsay. Charles Tansley, the young protégé of her husband, unburdens himself of his hard-luck story: 'He had wanted to tell her everything about himself' (24). She had first confided in him the story of Mr Carmichael's 'unfortunate marriage', with the comment that 'he should have been a great philosopher'. In reading this as a parable of proper relations between the sexes (and not, for example, noticing its ironic reference to Mrs Ramsay's own case, where the very dependence of Mr Ramsay, rather than the marriage's ending, is allegedly what has restrained his philosophizing), Tansley is 'flattered':

> Charles Tansley revived. Insinuating, too, as she did the greatness of man's intellect, even in its decay, the subjection of all wives . . . to their husband's labours, she made him feel better pleased with himself than he had

> done yet, and he would have liked, had they taken a cab, for example, to have paid for it. As for her little bag, might he not carry that? . . . He would like her to see him, gowned and hooded, walking in a procession.
>
> (*TL*, 20)[6]

But the final result of 'that extraordinary emotion which had been growing all the walk' (24) is a revelation:

> In she came, stood for a moment silent . . . stood quite motionless for a moment against a picture of Queen Victoria wearing the blue ribbon of the Garter; when all at once he realised that it was this: it was this: – she was the most beautiful person he had ever seen.
>
> With stars in her eyes and veils in her hair, with cyclamen and wild violets – what nonsense was he thinking? She was fifty at least; she had eight children.
>
> (*TL*, 25)

Momentarily the virgin, the queen and the mother coalesce into a mute image which makes the man something more than what he took himself previously to be: 'for the first time in his life Charles Tansley felt an extraordinary pride' (25). The woman's perfection and summation of every part establishes the man's identity.

It is the asymmetry of Freud's 'phase apart' that now points the way towards a consideration of the difference in the developments of boys and girls. For if the metaphors of journey, destination, progression – indeed, of 'development' itself in so far as the word implies determinate stages towards an end already known – are useful in thinking of the case of the man, they are less obviously applied to that of the woman imagined as the sustaining object of the gaze from the window. It was the realization of this asymmetry, prompted by the criticisms of other analysts including women, which led Freud, in what can appear retroactively as his own logical 'line' of intellectual development, to consider what was different in the girl's development to what is called femininity rather than to assume it as a progression along parallel lines to the boy's development to what is called masculinity.

It would seem that girls are placed in a structurally untenable position in so far as the main line of human development is concerned. For if subjectivity is figured by the place on the train, with the mother in the distance, left behind and idealized, but women in general devalued and despised for their lack of the attribute of masculinity, then women are effectively put in two places at once, both of which are undesirable. The third possibility is the place on the train, as part of the 'procession', but that is by definition deemed unwomanly as being reserved for men. The difficulty of reaching 'femininity' is emphasized by Freud when he speaks of no less than three possible 'lines of development' for girls after they have understood the meaning of sexual difference. Only one of these lines goes to 'normal' femininity (heterosexuality and motherhood); the other two, frigidity and homosexuality, each represent different versions of the refusal of the 'normal' feminine position.

'Anatomy is destiny', so often taken as the Freudian condemnation of women to a conventionally feminine fate, is rather the marking of the way that determinate social meanings are arbitrarily imposed upon subjects of either anatomical sex, and in far less tenable ways for the woman. Freud's account of the trials of the girl on her way to what is prescribed as normal femininity makes her development sound like a switchback railway journey thwarted with upheavals and potential reversals at every turn.[7] As has often been pointed out, these very difficulties can be taken as a kind of allegory of the impossibility for 'woman' of finding an approximate identity to match – to challenge and to fit in with – that of the masculine scenario which has already put her in certain contradictory positions. Masculine identity is permanently under threat, but 'femininity' never has the pretence to any positive content to begin with.

Mrs Ramsay seems to others the image of fulfilled womanhood, but does not sustain the equanimity she constantly proffers to assuage their doubts and floundering: 'For the most part, oddly enough, she must admit that she felt this thing that she called life terrible, hostile, and quick to pounce on you if you gave it a chance' (92). Her perpetual mothering represents for her the only way of holding at bay

'this thing' that is always ready to spring. 'She would have liked always to have had a baby' (90), and her demand upon others 'to say that people must marry, people must have children' (93) is said to emanate not from assurance but from a negotiation of what would otherwise be despair. Mrs Ramsay's own capacity to ease the sufferings of those around her is exposed as resting on her acknowledgement that the alleviation is only a patching over of a fundamental discord:

> She had often the feeling, Why must they grow up and lose it all? And then she said to herself, brandishing her sword at life, Nonsense. They will be perfectly happy. And here she was, she reflected, feeling life rather sinister again, making Minta marry Paul Rayley.
>
> (*TL*, 92)

The incompatibility of the marital relations upon which Mrs Ramsay nonetheless so vehemently insists is brought to the surface in the story she reads to James of the Fisherman's wife:

> Flounder, flounder, in the sea
> Come, I pray thee, here to me;
> For my wife, good Ilsabil,
> Wills not as I'd have her will.
>
> (*TL*, 87)

'"Well, what does she want then?" said the Flounder' (87), echoing – or anticipating – Freud's famous formulation. What he, Mr Ramsay, would have her will, she tries to will, and yet there remains a discrepancy after she has 'satisfied' him, after 'there throbbed through her . . . the rapture of successful creation' (61) which seems then to create or to comfort her too:

> Every throb of this pulse seemed, as he walked away, to enclose her and her husband, and to give to each that solace which two different notes, one high, one low, struck together, seem to give each other as they combine. Yet, as the resonance died, and she turned to the Fairy Tale again, Mrs Ramsay felt not only exhausted in body

> . . . but also there tinged her physical fatigue some faintly disagreeable sensation with another origin.
>
> (*TL*, 61)

Mrs Ramsay is 'discomposed' (62) by the 'disagreeable sensation' which itself has more than one part: not liking the public aspect of 'his coming to her like that, openly' for reassurance (62); not liking 'to feel finer than her husband' (61); 'not being entirely sure' (61) that he is as fine as she tells him he is to soothe him. Rather than 'the entire joy, the pure joy, of the two notes sounding together', the outcome of the exchange reminds her of a discordance, of what she calls (in the latest psychological language) 'the inadequacy of human relationships' (62). The image of perfect complementarity and reciprocity betwen the sexes shows itself to mask a basic disunity of parts that in fact do not fit, either within her or between the two of them.

If Mrs Ramsay endeavours to preserve the spectacle of the composure of feminine and masculine relationships, Lily Briscoe is placed outside this structure, fascinated by it but resisting incorporation into it as a woman who, in Mrs Ramsay's scheme, should marry Mr Bankes. Against Mrs Ramsay's urging that 'an unmarried woman has missed the best of life' (77), and Charles Tansley's running insistence that 'women can't paint, women can't write' (75), Lily 'would urge her own exemption from the universal law' (77); and this makes her, as when she is about to fail to give Mr Ramsay the solace he demands of her, 'not a woman' (226): 'That man, she thought, her anger rising in her, never gave; that man took. She, on the other hand, would be forced to give. Mrs Ramsay had given. Giving, giving, giving, she had died' (223).

In making of Lily a cultural and sexual rebel against 'the universal law', the novel seems to place her as the antithesis to Mrs Ramsay, whose energies are dedicated to the maintenance of all that Lily repudiates in her prescribed sexual destiny. Yet from another point of view, as has often been pointed out, their projects are analogous. The unification or bringing together of disparate things, of the 'discomposed', which Mrs Ramsay seeks to achieve by marryings and motherings, is also what Lily attempts in the field of art:

> Mrs Ramsay making of the moment something permanent (as in another sphere Lily herself tried to make of the moment something permanent) – this was of the nature of a revelation. In the midst of chaos there was shape; this eternal passing and flowing was struck into stability.
>
> (*TL*, 241)

This 'revelation' itself stands out in the narrative as a 'moment' to give coherence, a nodal point perhaps upon which to base a general interpretation of *To the Lighthouse*. Such a view lends itself readily to being brought into connection with Woolf's own interest in and endorsement of a particular modernist conception of the function of art: that the work of art makes in its own autonomous medium the unity which in the world itself is lacking. In the biographical reading of the Lily/Mrs Ramsay connection/opposition, Lily, like Virginia Stephen, represents the virginal artist daughter of the Victorian 'Angel in the House', moving tentatively away from the restrictions on female expectations to become what Mrs Ramsay thinks of as 'an independent little creature' (29). This parallel is borne out by the statements in Woolf's memoirs and her diary indicating that the writing of *To the Lighthouse* finally routed or put to rest the ghost of a too angelic mother who had haunted her since her death, when Virginia was only thirteen.

But it could be argued that the moment of unity, the apparently resolved triple sequence of times collected together in the completion of Lily Briscoe's picture, only emphasizes all the more strongly the underlying lack of harmony in 'human relationships', as in the art or institutions which attempt to cover over their 'inadequacy'. This is the alternative I have stressed in examining what undermines the unity of the most apparently unifying or unified of characters and episodes in the novel. But this is not then to argue that it is more 'adequate' to posit a general flux and fragmentation than a final unification. Rather, *To the Lighthouse* explores both the insistence and the untenability of the prevailing constructions of masculine and feminine identities, showing how the two are neither complementary, making a whole, nor ever reached in their imaginary completion by individuals of either sex. In particular, the conquering hero and the angel in the house are (masculine) fantasies, and it is in relation to them that men and women have to take up their parts, more or less adequately.

The three sections of *To the Lighthouse* are distinguished by different forms of temporality. The first and third focus, as often in Woolf's novels, on a single day and the associative links which connect it, in the consciousnesses of the characters and along the narrative line, to other times and places. The 'present moment' is divided and encompasses more than one time, and this effect is multiplied by the number of characters in such a way that their coming together as a group – for instance, in the dinner party scene – constitutes only a tenuous and ephemeral connection of many heterogeneous parts. Woolf uses the classical structure of a tragedy, with the action taking place in the course of a single day, to unwind the schematic outlines according to which persons, lives and events appear as comprehensible and consistent. The multiple layers of the day and the question of the position from which the narrator sees what she sees detract from the plausibility of a straightforward narrative, which might be characterized as a confidence in asserting or retracing the single way in which 'one thing led to another' (*BA*, 47).[8]

The middle section, 'Time Passes', makes Mrs Ramsay's death parenthetical, literally, to a general lack of differentiation from which identifiable human agency is absent, except for the ambivalent questioning of 'sea airs' (*TL*, 195), or the half-acknowledged place of the narrator:

> Night after night, summer and winter, the torment of storms, the arrow-like stillness of fine weather, held their court without interference. Listening (had there been anyone to listen) from the upper rooms of the empty house, only gigantic chaos streaked with lightning could have been heard tumbling and tossing.
>
> (*TL*, 202)

In this part, 'time passing' is represented rather as cyclical repetition than as the multiple story lines or criss-cross networks – to the past, and to other places – of a day. Natural rhythms take precedence over the appeal to any kind of progression or linear development: there is no specificity of a differentiated past or elsewhere structuring the present. But the half-acknowledged narrator also identifies the abandoned house as a kind of aesthetic image of natural, self-contained peace:

> So loveliness reigned and stillness, and together made the shape of loveliness itself, a form from which life had parted; solitary like a pool at evening, far distant, seen from a train window, vanishing so quickly that the pool, pale in the evening, is scarcely robbed of its solitude, though once seen.
>
> (*TL*, 195)

Neither of these two forms of temporality, or atemporality – the changelessness of the 'form', 'the shape of loveliness', or the repeated movements of a chaotic nature – apparently bears any relation to the linearity identified as masculine: they are like obverse sides against which it appears as an arbitrary imposition.

The other kinds of time – that of night and day, of waves, of seasons and years, or that of still form, signify no progression but the bareness of natural cycles, permanent recurrence and alternation, or else static completeness. It is these times which are often associated with femininity as cyclical and 'reproductive', or as iconic and eternal, and which are differentiated in *To the Lighthouse* from the arbitrary sequences of masterful 'masculine' temporality.

Yet in terms of the sexual structuring of subjectivity, this difference is far from absolute: it is not a dualism of two unrelated types. As with the interconnection of repetition and linearity in the keyboard simile, the 'shape of loveliness itself', likened to a pool glimpsed from a train window, acquires its meaning in relation to the distance and direction of the place from which it is seen. What appears as the pure origin of life in Mrs Ramsay ('this delicious fecundity' (58)) is so only by virtue of its capacity to symbolize the antithesis of the end-directed cultural purposes of 'the fatal sterility of the male' (58). It is at once the basis of meaning to authenticate the otherwise indefinite and wavering series of A to Z, and a means of comfort, representing an attempted restoration of infantile dependence and centrality. It also represents freedom from the 'failure' (58) which threatens to engulf from the point at which he joins the line of ambitious males headed and herded towards the letter R and beyond. The image of the succouring, nurturing woman serves to supply – and necessarily to fail to supply – the gap betwen R and Z, making up for the man's inevitable incapacity to get to the end of his line.

The absoluteness of the distinction between different times is also undermined in other ways. The repetitive work of the old women on the decaying house prevents rather than inducing a return to a natural state – 'the whole house would have plunged to the depths to lie upon the sands of oblivion' (209) – and is thus eminently a cultural enterprise. As if to underline this almost ironically, the restoration work is precipitated by the women's receipt of an imperious letter from the remnants of the Ramsay family: 'All of a sudden, would Mrs McNab see that the house was ready, one of the young ladies wrote' (209). This brings Mrs McNab close to what Mr Ramsay abstracts into the possible 'eternal necessity' of 'the liftman in the Tube' (67) than to a figure for the eternal feminine. But Mrs McNab's work against the dereliction of the house is also similar in form to the time pattern of Mrs Ramsay's life of dailiness. For the latter, 'the monotonous fall of the wave on the beach' (27) is either consoling or admonitory, warning 'her whose day had slipped past in one quick doing after another that it was all ephemeral as a rainbow' (28). So again, the clear division of different modes of temporality is made more complicated. The beat of the waves is not only a soothing return to cradle songs: it can also signify a forward march towards an end whose approach measures the dissipation of wasted days. The forms of feminine subjectivity cannot be separated from their position in relation to the governing order of masculine temporality.

If the 'Time Passes' section of *To the Lighthouse* figures as the antithesis against which the man's letters appear in sharpest outline and opposition, the first and third parts also – but differently – depart from that line, showing its multiple layers and complex crossings and intersections, like Mrs Ramsay's knitting. So different a view of the narrative line – without a place of mastery, and resembling a network or imbrication of many times, places, memories and fantasies – could be said to be feminine in that it looks beyond – just glimpses further than – the certainties of the recognizable, single line. If this is what constitutes the difference of modernist from realist narrative, it might also be what makes modernism in a certain sense 'feminine'.[9] For the time being, that 'feminine' is so by virtue of its pursuing different, less direct lines from those identified as masculine: by its moving away from what it regards, from another position, as the false neutrality and universality of the principal, masculine line.

To the Lighthouse makes evident the mapping of human subjectivity in terms of figurations inseparable from sexual difference, and it also shows the lack of fit, the 'phase apart', entailed by the discrepancy between the train of masculinity and the various outsider positions into which the woman is cast:

> ('Nature has but little clay,' said Mr Bankes once, much moved by her voice on the telephone, though she was only telling him a fact about a train, 'like that of which she moulded you.' He saw her at the end of the line very clearly Greek, straight, blue-eyed. How incongruous it seemed to be telephoning to a woman like that . . .)
>
> (*TL*, 46–7)

The woman moves the man to a poetic language quite different from the factual language of timetables. He imagines her as a Greek statue or goddess, returning backwards along a cultural line where artistic and feminine purity can be clearly seen, and which is marked by pathos through its necessary difference from the here and now associated with the mechanical lines of the railway and the phone. 'How incongruous to be telephoning to a woman like that' could be taken to condense all the features of the unparallel lines of masculine and feminine journeys. Just as the simile of the train passenger contrasted the straight progression along an arbitrary line with the image of the woman as restorer or giver of meaning, so Mr Bankes casts the lady in a mould of aesthetic perfection and endows her with the function of making up for the mechanical and routinized lines in the modern world.

The eventual arrival at the lighthouse, and the eventual completion or composition of Lily Briscoe's picture of James and Mrs Ramsay, are so belated in the novel as to put in question the very progression of which their achievement appears, at length, as a kind of formal culmination. This is no Z at the end of the alphabet, but rather the discovery of a different kind of line, contrary to the 'doomed expedition' (57) ordained for the forward march of masculine history. How to represent a more complex feminine or feminist temporality, against the simple lines of sequential progress, is one of the questions of *Mrs Dalloway*.

5 Thinking Forward Through Mrs Dalloway's Daughter

How far have women come? To answer such a question, it would be necessary to establish where women meant or were meant to go, to know their destination, and that of feminism. In *Three Guineas*, notoriously, Woolf looks forward at one point to a time when the word 'feminist' will have ceased to exist. In the context, the concern is with 'the right to earn a living' (*TG*, 101): at the end of the line, feminism has done its work when women have become eligible to enter the professions on the same basis as men. But elsewhere, it is not at all clear what for Woolf would constitute the 'end' of feminism: its purpose or its dissolution, as the movement reaches its goal.

The point about equality of opportunity may well itself be made tongue in cheek: while granting the symbolic significance of the change, Woolf has been quick to point out just how few women's names are actually to be found among the lists of professions accorded a place in the latest edition of *Whitaker's Almanac*, and to speculate as to the reasons for 'this curious deficiency or disparity' (*TG*, 47). Further on, she considers the possibility that the 'difference' of men and women (*TG*, 104), whether a product of nature or of education, may in fact render inappropriate women's direct participation in anti-war activities (which is the problem that forms the starting point of her argument).

The question of women's aims and destinations as a group is thus rapidly linked for Woolf with the question of what a 'woman' is, or of what a woman would be in a society not ordered along patriarchal lines. In 'Mr Bennett and Mrs

Brown', we followed Woolf's movement through several possible definitions of feminism: in terms of equal rights to travel on the train that has so far been masculine in its direction; as a buried but natural difference presently suppressed by masculine culture; as a protestation of women's difference from men's representations of them, leaving open the question of what, if any, difference might eventually emerge on the other side of the process of counter-argument. In *A Room of One's Own*, Woolf's narrator protested sharply against nineteenth-century feminist anger as manifested in Eliot and Charlotte Brontë, and against the conscious gendering of a literary text: 'It is fatal for anyone who writes to think of their sex' (*ROO*, 99). But she also invoked such sexual consciousness as positive, suggesting that 'we' do and should 'think back through our mothers, if we are women' (*ROO*, 72–3).

Woolf's equivocations on these issues are not fortuitous, nor are they in need of final settlement. Her texts' endorsements of what are now demarcated as incompatible and conflicting feminist stances leads to confusion when she is claimed as a wholehearted subscriber to one or other of them, and the literary programmes that each is taken to imply. But the demand to pin her down to a definite position closes off just those questions which Woolf's texts never do determine once and for all, insisting contrary to many warnings on the part of her narrators and her characters that she be 'this . . . or that' (*MD*, 9). Just as Mrs Brown never actually arrives at the Waterloo terminus in the centre of London (and who knows whether she wants to get there anyway?), so Woolf leaves open the question of where 'women' are going as necessarily unanswerable. To be sure of the destination would be to put a premature end to the question, to have settled down already as if the journey were over. Instead, she keeps open many lines, as a response to what she always acknowledges as the impossibly complex network of determinations of women's difference; and, by a further connection, as the difficulty of knowing which questions to put in order to understand that difference. Many of these issues about the destinations and definitions of feminism and femininity come to the fore in *Mrs Dalloway*. They are posed in terms both of the arrival (or not) at a final, clear-cut identity, and of the difference in the directions available to two generations of women, a mother and a daughter.

When Elizabeth Dalloway steps out and takes the bus up the Strand on a fine June day in 1923, everything seems to suggest that she is the bearer of new opportunities for her sex, a woman who will be able to go further than her mother, still bound to the conventional femininity of the Victorian Angel in the House denounced by Woolf in 'Professions for Women'.[1] Elizabeth indulges in an excursion of independent fancy through the streets of London during which she is associated with the omnipotence attributed to the means of transport:

> Suddenly Elizabeth stepped forward and most competently boarded the omnibus, in front of everybody. She took a seat on top. The impetuous creature – a pirate – started forward, sprang away; she had to hold the rail to steady herself, for a pirate it was, reckless, unscrupulous, bearing down ruthlessly, circumventing dangerously, boldly snatching a passenger, or ignoring a passenger, squeezing eel-like and arrogant in between, and then rushing insolently all sails spread up Whitehall.
>
> (*MD*, 120)

The movement through unfamiliar parts of the city inspires Elizabeth with ideas of a life quite different from that of her mother, criticized by Peter Walsh as 'the perfect hostess' (56):

> Oh, she would like to go a little farther. Another penny, was it, to the Strand? Here was another penny, then. She would go up the Strand.
>
> She liked people who were ill. And every profession is open to the women of your generation, said Miss Kilman. So she might be a doctor. She might be a farmer. . . . It was quite different here from Westminster, she thought, getting off at Chancery Lane. It was so serious; it was so busy. In short, she would like to have a profession. She would become a doctor, a

> farmer, possibly go into Parliament if she found it necessary, all because of the Strand.
>
> (*MD*, 121)

Elizabeth's imaginative venture could be taken as a positive sign of women's progress: she is driven by ambitions beyond the ken of women thirty years before, and unencumbered by the pressure of masculine interference. Rather, in that she may become an MP, like Richard Dalloway, she identifies with the possibilities of a paternal profession.

No bar is placed on her rambling exploration, which suggests a difference from a related Victorian text which, as mentioned in chapter 1, is cited, and censured, in *A Room of One's Own*. 'That is an awkward break', announces the edgy narrator (*ROO*, 66), who wishes that what seems to be Grace Poole's laugh did not intrude upon what then seems all the more defensive a protest on behalf of women's 'restlessness' and right to wider experience. The chapter of *Jane Eyre* from which Woolf quotes begins with the optimistic statement that 'The promise of a smooth career, which my first introduction to Thornfield Hall seemed to pledge, was not belied on a longer acquaintance with the place and its inmates';[2] but the limits to the satisfaction afforded by that career appear on the very same page:

> I longed for a power of vision which might overpass that limit; which might reach the busy world, towns, regions full of life I had heard of but never seen; . . . I desired more of practical experience than I possessed. . . .
>
> Who blames me? Many, no doubt, and I shall be called discontented. I could not help it; the restlessness was in my nature; it agitated me to pain sometimes. Then my sole relief was to walk along the corridor of the third storey, backwards and forwards, safe in the silence and solitude of the spot, and allow my mind's eye to dwell on whatever bright visions rose before it – and, certainly, they were many and glowing; to let my heart be heaved by the exultant movement, which, while it swelled it in trouble, expanded it with life; and, best of all, to open my inward ear to a tale that was never ended

> – a tale my imagination created, and narrated continuously; quickened with all of incident, life, fire, feeling, that I desired and had not in my actual existence.[3]

Woolf's own citation of the passage beginning 'Who blames me?' breaks off awkwardly after 'pain sometimes'. The focus is then on a 'restlessness' detached from both the desire for 'practical' experience and sights of 'the busy world', and the imaginary 'relief' of the 'bright visions' and the 'tale that was never ended', supplying 'all of incident, life, fire, feeling' missing in actuality.

It is these omissions which make possible Woolf's criticism of gratuitous expressions of anger by women writers. But it is as if the eliminated parts return in Woolf's own novel to structure her twentieth-century rewriting of the Victorian spinster's prospects, where every element is included *except* the anger. For Elizabeth Dalloway there is no censorious Beadle or Woolf to put a stop to her reverie. A practical aspect to her dreams is suggested in the repeated, tangible fact that women can now enter the professions: Elizabeth is presumably in no danger of having to become an impecunious orphan governess, *à la* Jane Eyre, and thus (in Woolf's terms) has no need to give vent to the anger condemned as a flaw in her predecessor. So it might indeed seem that what was mere fantasy for a nineteenth-century woman, an imagining of liberty so futile as to be psychologically debilitating, has now become a realistic possibility. Whereas Jane Eyre dreams out from a distant rural rooftop, Elizabeth Dalloway is already on top of the bus, travelling through the city in which she may well fulfil her ambitions.

This point could be reinforced by placing Elizabeth's London adventure alongside that of another Brontë heroine, Lucy Snowe. On her way to be a teacher in Villette in Belgium, Lucy stops for a night in London and explores the City with the same passion that grips her twentieth-century literary descendant:

> Descending, I went wandering whither chance might lead, in a still ecstacy of freedom and enjoyment; and I got – I know not how – I got into the heart of city life. I saw and felt London at last: I got into the Strand; I went

> up Cornhill; I mixed with the life passing along; I dared the perils of crossings. To do this, and to do it utterly alone, gave me, perhaps an irrational, but a real pleasure. Since those days, I have seen the West-end, the parks, the fine squares; but I love the city far better. The city seems to me so much more in earnest: its business, its rush, its roar, are such serious things, sights, and sounds. The city is getting its living – the West-end but enjoying its pleasure.[4]

Lucy makes the same distinction as Elizabeth between the 'serious' city business of 'getting a living' and the relative triviality of other parts: 'the West-end *but* enjoying its pleasure'. Like Elizabeth, she travels at random, 'whither chance might lead'; and for Lucy too, the solitary discovery of unknown regions is itself 'a real pleasure'.

Yet further on, crossing the Channel, she will correct her sunny speculations about a European future 'grand with imperial promise' for herself:

> Cancel the whole of that, if you please, reader – or rather let it stand, and draw thence a moral – an alternative, text-hand copy –
>
> Day-dreams are delusions of the demon.[5]

And previously, the decision to venture was represented as anything but a wide open prospect:

> A strong, vague persuasion, that it was better to go forward than backward, and that I *could* go forward – that a way, however narrow and difficult, would in time open, predominated over other feelings: its influence hushed them so far, that at last I became sufficiently tranquil to be able to say my prayers and seek my couch.[6]

Lucy's humble future in Villette is more a response to necessity than the fulfilment of a far-flung desire for a wider experience, the 'day-dreams' whose dangerous and unsettling effects must be censored for the sake of sanity.

The apparent contrast in the outlooks of Brontë governesses and Dalloway daughters is reinforced by a difference of social class. The penniless Jane Eyre and Lucy Snowe do what is decently possible and financially unavoidable for the respectable poor; Elizabeth Dalloway comes of Establishment stock, and has herself been educated by an impoverished exile. This is the formidable Miss Kilman, who has had none of her pupil's chances, and whose bitterness is perhaps, by caricature, another Woolfian jab at the anger of the Brontë heroine. It is as if Miss Kilman is a nineteenth-century specimen rudely repackaged and sent on, complete with a religious faith whose anachronism in the secular Dalloway society is underlined by its fundamentalist excess. Such a character, like the suffrage workers of *Night and Day* and like 'Miss Julia Hedge, the feminist' in *Jacob's Room*, is one of a fairly numerous sisterhood in Woolf's novels.[7]

But these complexities should already suggest that the passage from the nineteenth to the twentieth century is not so direct or progressive as it may at first have seemed. For while Elizabeth Dalloway's daydreams are certainly more realizable in one sense than Lucy Snowe's or Jane Eyre's, they are no less marked, like Jane Eyre's, by a fantasy of transgression, which is set in a close relation to the various familial and educational influences on her.

The bus trip is initially an escape from the by now unbearable company of the same Miss Kilman who is the origin of her ideas of female aspiration. But Elizabeth's attachment to her, and in particular this afternoon's outing which began as a visit to the Army and Navy Stores, is in part in defiance of her mother, to whom it is a cause of distress. Professional plans are explicitly conceived as anti-maternal: she is 'quite determined, whatever her mother might say, to become either a farmer or a doctor' (*MD*, 122). And this despite the fact that her mother apparently considers the idea of Dalloway professional women as a long-established tradition, not a revolutionary breakthrough or breaking away:

> But then, of course, there was in the Dalloway family the tradition of public service. Abbesses, principals, head mistresses, dignitaries, in the republic of women – without being brilliant, any of them, they were that.
> (*MD*, 122)

For Clarissa, female authority is a matter 'of course'. Elizabeth's professional fantasy is thus ironic in that it functions as an escape from what she perceives as the constraints of two supporters of professions for women, the mother and the governess. And Elizabeth readily returns for the time being to her domestic calling as a good, civilized daughter: 'She must go home. She must dress for dinner. But what was the time? – where was a clock?' (122). The novel's finale places her at the side of her father, with whose professional achievements she earlier courted an identification. Now, instead, she is seen by him, unrecognized at first, as a beautiful young woman. This does not make her her father's equal or surrogate, but effectively returns her to the position of the idealized object of what she dismissed before as 'trivial chatterings (comparing women to poplar trees)' (121).

Elizabeth's destiny, then, is far from certain in either its evaluation or its outcome. Her predicament places her alternatives as between the possibility of participation in the centres of masculine power, as 'unscrupulous' and 'arrogant' as the bus (120), and what appears as an ignominious succumbing to a 'trivial' femininity as the object of male admiration. The incompatibility of the two is pathetically suggested by the scene of Miss Kilman's resentful and random purchase of a petticoat in the department store.

But Elizabeth's story is not, of course, the primary focus of *Mrs Dalloway*. That is part of what makes it so innovative a text, in that the heroine is the woman of fifty and not her eighteen-year-old daughter on the brink of courtship. For the most visible subject of the novel is the insistent re-enactment for the older woman of the romantic drama which according to most of literature should have been 'settled' once and for all thirty years before, with her choice of Richard Dalloway as a husband.

In a stimulating essay on *Mrs Dalloway*, Elizabeth Abel says that the novel 'demonstrates the common literary prefiguration of psychoanalytic doctrine, which can retroactively articulate patterns implicit in the literary text'.[8] Recapitulating the difficulty of the development towards 'normal' heterosexual femininity as described by Freud, Abel reads the conclusion as Clarissa's belated acceptance, thirty years after the events, of her 'choice' of Richard over the pre-Oedipal female bonding of her relationship with Sally Seton.

The particular inflection in *Mrs Dalloway* of such a claim for the prefiguring of psychoanalytic theories can be pointed up, once again, by a comparison with Brontë. In *Villette*, there is a literal recovery of the original family setting when Lucy Snowe awakens after her lapse of consciousness to find herself once again surrounded by the relatives familiar from her childhood, magically removed to the same foreign city; which then leads to the beginning of what she imagines as a romantic relationship with her attractive male cousin. In *Mrs Dalloway*, such a structure is reinscribed in the form of the literal reappearance of many of the chief and minor actors in the decisive period of Clarissa's youth: Ellie Henderson, Aunt Helena – 'for Miss Helena Parry was not dead' (158) – Sally Seton, and above all Peter Walsh. Yet this functions not as a new start in the form of new romantic commitments, but as a means of negotiating what are shown to have been insistently present rememberings of that time in the minds of Clarissa and Peter throughout the day and, by implication, throughout their lives.

Sally's passionate kiss, interrupted by Peter and another man, is centred in Abel's reading as representing the impossible and abandoned alternative to the nun-like chastity Clarissa has instead adopted in becoming Mrs Richard Dalloway. Her daughter's liaison with Doris Kilman, in contrast, is a more ambivalent female bonding, since it is described in terms of conflicting determinations and structured in relation to a revolt from her own mother, the first, and female, object of love. The 'purity' (32) of the relationship with Sally stands out all the more by comparison; but it is so in virtue of its status as a memory, an old wives' tale which figures in retrospect for Clarissa as the lost idyll of youth before she married and moved to London. What the novel suggests, then, is not so much the purer status of love between women as the giving up implicit in the turn to maturity, in this case heterosexual. For as Abel points out, Clarissa's feelings for women are themselves infiltrated by masculine and feminine imagery: 'she did undoubtedly then feel what men felt' (30).

Peter Walsh also features in Clarissa's reminiscences (as she in his), representing the romantic hero rejected in favour of the conventionality personified by the Conservative Member of Parliament.[9] She reacts after Peter's unexpected morning visit:

> If I had married him, this gaiety would have been mine all day!
>
> It was all over for her. The sheet was stretched and the bed narrow. She had gone up into the tower alone and left them blackberrying in the sun.
>
> (*MD*, 43)

Again, it is not so much implied that Clarissa should have married Peter really, as that the choice of a life as Mrs Dalloway made way for the idealization of the two other lovers thereby given up: that it was not a one-and-only choice and as a result has been written over, throughout its long duration, with memories and imaginings of the other lives neglected for that of the 'perfect hostess'.

The instabilities and overlappings of individual identity are constantly, repeatedly emphasized in *Mrs Dalloway*. Clarissa herself 'would not say of any one in the world now that they were this or were that' (9); the ending, with her reaction to the suicide of a man she has never heard of, reinforces a connection that the narrative, with its separate account of the drama of Septimus and Lucrezia Warren Smith, has implicitly made all along. Her objection, in the same context, to the psychiatrist's doctrine of 'Proportion' ('Sir William said he never spoke of "madness"; he called it not having a sense of proportion' (86)) parallels Septimus' own.

The lack of settlement or of fixed identity in Clarissa's life stands out also in its difference from the order and regularity – the daily 'proportions' – indicated by the repeated chiming of Big Ben. The intoning of the hours is associated with the authority of national and other institutions: with what Paul Ricoeur, following Nietzsche, calls 'monumental' time.[10] Ricoeur links this with the symbolic force of the figure of royalty passing in anonymous majesty through London during Clarissa's shopping expedition; or with the enigmatically suggestive advertising slogan written on high and eagerly deciphered by the crowd whom it equally draws together and hails from the sky with its brand-name riddle.

Such emblems of power are fully implicated in this novel, as habitually in Woolf, with masculinity institutionalized and imposing. Here Peter Walsh looks on:

> Boys in uniform, carrying guns, marched with their eyes ahead of them, marched, their arms stiff, and on their faces an expression like the letters of a legend written round the base of a statue praising duty, gratitude, fidelity, love of England.
>
> (*MD*, 46–7)

Big Ben keeps in time with this lifeless national parade of conformity and 'discipline' (47):

> The sound of Big Ben striking the half-hour struck out between them with extraordinary vigour, as if a young man, strong, indifferent, inconsiderate, were swinging dumb-bells this way and that.
>
> (*MD*, 44)

It is as if the highlighting of the time, almost a refrain with the repetition in the narrative of exact forms of words, brings to the fore the artifice of the naturalized structure within which individual lives and times are differentiated. A similar effect is produced in *The Waves* by the poetic interludes describing the movement of the sun, and making the analogy between a life, or six lives, and a day. But whereas that time is represented as the natural framework of a recurring solar movement, in *Mrs Dalloway* the use of the clock and the specification of hours and half hours proceeding in order from one to twelve and from a.m. to p.m. makes time more linear than circular, emphasizing the man-made, cultural arbitrariness of the 'twenty-four' hours into which the day is divided.

In *The Waves*, it is Louis, the would-be master and maker of global order, whose time is exactly that of the mechanical clock:

> I have fused my many lives into one; I have helped by my assiduity and decision to score those lines on the map there by which the different parts of the world are laced

> together. I love punctually at ten to come into my room; ... I love the telephone with its lip stretched to my whisper, and the date on the wall; and the engagement book. Mr Prentice at four; Mr Eyres at four-thirty.
>
> (*W*, 113)

Louis's time is not dominant in *The Waves*, but placed in relation to those of the five other 'characters'. He stands at the most 'civilized' point of a polarity whose other extreme is represented in the 'natural' time of Susan, the mother and country-dweller.

In *Mrs Dalloway*, the imperial Big Ben time is undermined not only by the discontinuous temporalities of the various characters and the double time which they live, but more literally by the belated chiming of other clocks which challenge or mock the precision of Big Ben's time-keeping. The clock with a feminine name follows after:

> Ah, said St Margaret's, like a hostess who comes into her drawing-room on the very stroke of the hour and finds her guests there already. I am not late. No, it is precisely half-past eleven, she says. Yet, though she is perfectly right, her voice, being the voice of the hostess, is reluctant to inflict its individuality. Some grief for the past holds it back; some concern for the present. It is half-past eleven, she says, and the sound of St Margaret's glides into the recesses of the heart and buries itself in ring after ring of sound, like something alive which wants to confide itself, to disperse itself, to be, with a tremor of delight, at rest – like Clarissa herself, thought Peter Walsh, coming downstairs on the stroke of the hour in white.
>
> (*MD*, 45–6)

Via Peter's thoughts, the narrative makes the already suggested link with the 'hostess' Clarissa explicit, and adds to the connections of that term in Woolf's writing. In 'Mr Bennett and Mrs Brown', the novels of Bennett, Galsworthy and Wells were criticized for their resemblance to hostesses who never get beyond polite introductions to substantive communication. Here, on the other hand, the formalities of the doorstep are not so much prolonged as superfluous in the face of an apparent breach of convention, the guests being already installed. St Margaret's makes of the perfect hostess (there on the dot, and 'perfectly' right) the possibly less than perfect, denying what may be her tardiness. She loses in any case by the fact of asserting and acting on her different view: even if (according to the arbitration of some ultimate clock in the sky) it is actually she who is right, she has *de facto* renounced her status by failing to defer to her guests. So the feminine hostess cannot win: if perfect she is too perfect, merely polite; if other than polite, differing from her guests, she is imperfect.

In contrast to the 'indifference' of Big Ben, St Margaret's wants to connect. Neither wholly neutral nor wholly in the present, 'some grief for the past holds it back; some concern for the present'. It is 'like something alive which wants to confide itself, to disperse itself'. The syntax of this part of the sentence creates a gap between 'to be' and 'at rest', before 'Clarissa herself' appears, and invokes all the uncertainty of her own attitude to life: at once an active pursuit, in the creative 'gift' of her parties, and a retreat into her attic room, a wish like Septimus' to be finally at rest.

Such equivocations on the part of Clarissa/St Margaret's also render questionable her relation to the preceding peal of Big Ben. St Margaret's more doubtful ring could be seen as either complementary (the trivial following the serious, both making a well-tuned ensemble), or lightly mocking (the second bell sounding a gentle mimic), or challenging, by disrupting and detracting from his univocal, authoritative announcement.

The significance of the hostess as clock is thus far from single in its resonances. 'Clarissa herself' epitomizes the hostess/woman who barely, but just, finds a harmonious place within the sound and purview of recognized social forms. Whereas Septimus Smith is the extreme 'case' of someone who has lost all contact with the external, common orders of daily life and daily time, Clarissa is questionably situated like St Margaret's, neither within nor without, somewhere between utter differing and absolute conformity. She is close enough to sound or seem as if she simply echoes established authority, and distant enough for her chimes to verge on an expression of doubt or an ironic doubling.

Clarissa is both perfectly conventional in her role as lady and hostess and, at the same time, a misfit: *Mrs Dalloway* is all about the fact that she is still unresolved in a choice apparently completed a generation before. The calm security which is itself the conventional appearance of the hostess is undermined in so far as Clarissa is frequently in different times and places, remaking and reinforcing her preference for Richard over Peter, now structured as a clear-cut opposition between stability and adventure. Like Mrs Ramsay, to all appearances a model of maternal equilibrium, she is in reality anything but 'composed', except in the sense of being put together from disparate parts, as we shall see in more detail: 'she always had the feeling that it was very, very dangerous to live even one day' (*MD*, 9).

The same risky balance of subjectivity is suggested in *The Waves* in terms of the relation between collective and individual identity. The focus is not on the multiple directions which might have been taken by each of the six 'characters', but on their lack of fit with the world or with one another, these fundamental differences showing up the tenuous and transient nature of their moments of unity as a group. By using a narrative structure of straightforward sequence rather than retrospect, the period of childhood succeeded by the various stages from early adulthood through to late middle age, Woolf seems to cut out what is the principal concern of *Mrs Dalloway*. This is the degree to which an individual 'lifeline' or path is never single and given from the beginning, but is rather secured only by the turning away from or lack of access to other directions, which may continue to figure as powerful fantasies.

In *The Waves*, it is as if the characters are settled in their 'ways' from the start, or from particular determining moments (Susan's witnessing of Jinny's kissing Louis, for instance, or Louis's determination to overcome what he takes to be the disadvantages of his Australian accent). They also announce all along, with a clarity and consistency that is not to be doubted, what they want, what their failings are, how they view the world (Jinny has a limited 'hoard' of life as pleasure to consume, Neville seeks defensive fulfilment in privacy and love against the 'chaos' of the world outside; Louis sees the same chaos, but instead of retreating inwards seeks to convert it to order; and so on).

But the simplification in the delineation of character enables the issue to be raised at a different level. It is by comparisons between, not within, the speakers that differences appear in this novel, and the question of unification or its absence occurs at the level of their community, occasionally and momentarily assembled, rather than at the level of an individual shown to be herself or himself many-sided, made up of multiple parts.[11]

In *Mrs Dalloway*, the feminine charms and chimes of St Margaret's call up an instability of the hostess's identity which extends beyond Clarissa Dalloway to other characters. The novel treats with contempt those who are so simple as to fit in without a hitch with the imperial, patriarchal order of 'a young man, strong, indifferent, inconsiderate' (*MD*, 44). But such characters are not endowed with the young man's arrogance so much as with the stupidity of his 'dumb-bells'. Most outrageously, there is the Prime Minister at Clarissa's party: 'He looked so ordinary. You might have stood him behind a counter and bought biscuits – poor chap, all rigged up in gold lace' (152). But this patent insignificance in the flesh does nothing to dull the other guests' sense of 'this majesty passing; this symbol of what they all stood for, English society' (153). The courtly Hugh Whitbread has been 'afloat on the cream of English society for fifty-five years' (92), and 'little Mr Bowley', one of the gossips of *Jacob's Room* here making a brief reappearance, is 'sealed with wax over the deeper source of life'. He is 'unsealed' by a warm breeze coupled with the passing of the royal vehicle in the Mall, which 'lifted some flag flying' in his 'British breast' (*MD*, 19): but this unsealing, ironically, reveals only a deeper layer of pure Britishness.[12] All such completely standardized – flag-flying – characters are male; Richard Dalloway's respect for the symbols of civilization is contrasted with the cynicism of Peter Walsh, self-exiled from Britain and still looking for a woman to replace what he thinks he lost in Clarissa: as preoccupied by the decisive earlier period as is Clarissa herself.[13]

The theme of exile – again, a reinscription of a *Villette* motif – suggests further the self-separation of the more complicated characters: those whose non-conformity and non-integration sets them apart, so that they are always as if in two places or two times at once. Miss Kilman and Lucrezia Smith are the most obvious examples, the first of German origin, and the second – 'Why hadn't she stayed at home?' (25) – departed from Italy to become the wife of Septimus. Others are exiles in London from other parts of the country – either, like Lady Bruton or Clarissa, from grand country seats where they spent their childhood, or, like Maisie Johnson just arrived from Edinburgh and like Septimus himself, in order to seek fame or fortune in the big city. This generalized estrangement in London reinforces the metaphorical exile of all those characters who are not 'British' through and through, adding a geographical counterpart to the temporal division of present and past, the requirement to be definitely masculine or feminine as opposed to the remembered openness of childhood. It is manifested most of all in the case of the female vagrant looking 'as if she had flung herself on the earth, rid of all ties, to observe curiously, to speculate boldly, to consider the whys and the wherefores' (104). This extreme case stresses the positive advantages of exile, not being at home in the world being the outsider situation from which it is possible to 'speculate boldly'.

With her project of dispatching young people 'born of respectable parents' (97) to colonize Canada, Lady Bruton seems not so much an exile as one who exiles. Yet though 'power was hers, position, income' (100), this 'martial woman' (97) suffers from a deficiency which is attributed to her sex – 'she used to feel the futility of her own womanhood' (97) – and which apparently deprives her of the means of inditing letters to *The Times*. The disparity between Lady Bruton's ruthless projects and her feminine failings makes a comic exaggeration of the novel's suggestion of the incompatibility of masculine and feminine identities in the present form of their distinction. (Hugh Whitbread, specially imported to assist with the composition, supplies the lady's lack with gentlemanly discretion, 'drafting sentiments in alphabetical order of the highest nobility' (98), like an epistolary version of Mr Ramsay.)

Millicent Bruton's simple division between the domineering masculine and the helpless feminine provides another aspect to the figure of the hostess, in this case inviting two male guests specifically in order to make up for the only weak spot in what is otherwise exaggerated masculinity. In Clarissa, the hostess is rather an outward image of femininity as a perfect integrity belied by its difficult composition:

> She pursed her lips when she looked in the glass. It was to give her face point. That was her self – pointed; dart-like; definite. That was her self when some effort, some call on her to be her self, drew the parts together, she alone knew how different, how incompatible and composed so for the world only into one centre, one diamond, one woman who sat in her drawing-room and made a meeting-point, a radiancy no doubt in some dull lives.
>
> (*MD*, 34–5)

Only 'some call on her' temporarily co-ordinates what are otherwise 'incompatible', separate parts into what will then look like 'her self'. The 'one centre, one diamond, one woman' is herself effaced as simply the 'meeting-point' that irradiates and draws together other 'lives', like Percival the silent 'centre' of *The Waves*. And this effect of harmony, itself dispersed across three approximations, occurs only when she is most deliberately constructed, by 'some effort' integrated into a semblance of unity by another 'her' who is aware of the difference: 'she alone', distinct from the outer 'centre', 'she alone knew how different, how incompatible and composed so for the world only'.

The 'call' which demands this integration is unspecified in its origin. It produces at the same time the appearance of unity which conceals multiplicity, and the 'she alone', apart from it, whose knowledge of, and at another level from, the heterogeneity of the façade inaugurates a further separation. Given such fundamental divisions, constitutive of her very identity as 'one woman', there is no way of settling the nature of the 'perfect hostess', apparently so 'definite', when she is at home.

It is by this complicated route that Clarissa Dalloway's predicament returns as a question for her daughter. In the same way that, as Elizabeth Abel points out, the significant and unconcluded episode of Clarissa's youth appears to begin and end in late adolescence rather than infancy, Elizabeth Dalloway is a young woman without a past and with many possible future directions: 'Buses swooped, settled, were off – garish caravans, glistening with red and yellow varnish. But which should she get on to? She had no preferences' (120). Unlike her mother's period of hesitation at Bourton, Elizabeth's takes place in the city which can then figure forth the new urban opportunities not available to her mother's generation of women. But Elizabeth's fantasies are represented, as we have seen, as a form of rebellion against maternal wishes; and the narrator, sometimes via the thoughts of the mother, represents her as naïve: 'So she might be a doctor. She might be a farmer. Animals are often ill. She might own a thousand acres and have people under her. She would go and see them in their cottages' (121). This suggests that Elizabeth's professional ideas are childish rather than mature fantasies, and adds force to the hints that she may turn from them to the more usual feminine place she presently refuses: 'For it was beginning. Her mother could see that. The compliments were beginning' (120). Further, the difference between being an object of poetic idealization and being a professional is structured for Elizabeth as a mutually exclusive opposition of the 'trivial' to the 'serious'. For the time being, she places herself on the masculine side of that valuation, rather than seeking to modify its hierarchy or its terms of exclusion.

Mrs Dalloway makes visible the absence of unity behind the centred façade of 'a woman' deemed to be the emblem of such pacific completion – 'the perfect hostess', married for thirty years – and this then seems to pave the way for the unavoidable non-finality of any course that the daughter may come to take. The indeterminate places of both mother and daughter draw attention to the greater complexity of women's unroyal roads to a femininity that is always other than fully integrated; but also to a greater openness from their very lack of fit with the dominant masculine order. In the fictional '1923', Elizabeth like her mother is still subject to 'some call' upon her to live up to 'the compliments', and the city career she dreams of is marked as a 'serious' escape from a feminine triviality she rejects. It is because and not in spite of this stark division that her 'pioneer' venture into parts of London where Dalloways fear to tread ('For no Dalloways came down the Strand daily' (122)) may lead to the discovery of an identity which is formed otherwise than by the difference between the serious 'procession' of urban conformity and the angel or hostess in the house.

After looking at Woolf's different and interlocking analyses of the structure of sexual difference, the complex path to femininity and the possible future directions for women, we can now turn to see how her overtly feminist questions are linked to an understanding of biographical and historical narratives. In 'Mr Bennett and Mrs Brown', it was precisely in pretending to narrative neutrality that the male novelists turned out to be most insidiously askew. The next two chapters investigate the questions Woolf's texts raise about the representation first of biographical development (in *Jacob's Room*, where it is clear that assumptions of neutrality in the representation of character always in fact involve a covert masculine norm), and then of historical change (in *Roger Fry* and in *The Years*). In *Orlando*, as we shall see in chapter 8, Woolf puts these questions in the form of a parody of the conventions of coherence and narrative development in the writing of history and biography; while in *Between the Acts* (chapter 9), she shows the instability of language itself in the construction of collective fictions of history and identity.

6 Jacob's Type

> They were all young and some of them seemed to make a protest by their hair and dress, and something sombre and truculent in the expression of their faces, against the more normal type, who would have passed unnoticed in an omnibus or an underground railway.
>
> (*ND*, 46)

> The proximity of the omnibuses gave the outside passengers an opportunity to stare into each other's faces. Yet few took advantage of it. Each had his own business to think of. Each had his past shut in him like the leaves of a book known to him by heart; and his friends could only read the title, James Spalding, or Charles Budgeon, and the passengers going the opposite way could read nothing at all – save 'a man with a red moustache,' 'a young man in grey smoking a pipe.'
>
> (*JR*, 62)

Like the train, the 'omnibus' is often used in Woolf's novels to dramatize the complexity of the representation or 'reading' of character (including the observer's). This passage moves in several directions at once. Knowing a person is analogous to reading a book, and there are three stages or levels of reading: 'in depth' knowledge, 'by heart'; the simple title, similar to the proper name; and the short, cited phrase giving the sex and a single, visible attribute. The individual, who is the best and only comprehensive reader of herself or himself, consists of his 'business' and (or?) 'his past'.

There are no separate, self-consistent entities: each person also reads himself, even if adequately, and is thus made up of at least two parts, one reading or knowing the other (the business, the past). Auto-reading involves a reader and a text and is not radically distinguishable from reading other books, or others' books. While the passage at first sight implies that 'each' person has a full, inside knowledge of himself or herself, compared to which knowledge of others is only partial, the reading metaphor dispels this distinction by taking away the unity of the self-reader, and thereby puts into focus the partiality, in both senses, of any reading of another, including the reader.

The situation of 'outside passenger' thus passes by what is often laid out as an opposition between the representation of characters as types and the evocation of absolute, ineffable idiosyncrasy. An established mode of criticism, whose most famous exponent is probably Woolf's friend and contemporary E. M. Forster, makes a clear distinction between 'round' and 'flat' characters, or between the individual of 'depth' and the mere two-dimensional 'type'.[1] Such distinctions tend to be based on humanist assumptions: that all men (and sometimes all women) are, fundamentally, unique individuals, profound and many-sided, but that a writer's ineptitude, prejudice or conscious technique (in the case of comedy, for example) may lead to the production of 'wooden' characters without the capacity to seem like 'real people'. But in the passage above, reading in terms of any of the three levels proposed depends on the position of the observer, which is constantly shifting. The hypothesis of a concealed depth, a book in everyone awaiting its reader, is itself generated by the situation of the casual encounter, the confrontation – 'an opportunity to stare into each other's faces' – with another who is readable only in terms of superficial attributes readily translated into formulaic phrases. Thus, the anonymity exemplified by urban public transport reinforces rather than detracting from the 'rounded' wholeness associated with the private relationship which then figures as its polar opposite.

Jacob's Room, I shall try to suggest, is both an interrogation of the notion of individuality and, at the same time, a demonstration of the inescapability of 'typing' in the making – autobiographically and as perceived by others – of what is thought of as an individual self. Woolf does not posit, as an alternative to the idea of multiple individuals, each distinct, the hypothesis of a fixed classificatory order according to which individuals can be instantly recognized as one type or another. Rather, she looks at the ways in which processes of 'typing' necessarily go on all the time, and precede structurally what then appears to be the absolutely unique individual.

Like *Orlando* in a different mode, *Jacob's Room* satirizes the standard format of the biography of the exceptional man. First, it makes of Jacob less a unique hero than a nebulous absent centre, like Percival in *The Waves*, to be invested with whatever attributes are seen to be narratively appropriate. Jacob is more an object of others' interpretations and readings than an agent 'in his own right':

> But how far was he a mere bumpkin? How far was Jacob Flanders at the age of twenty-six a stupid fellow? It is no use trying to sum people up. One must follow hints, not exactly what is said, nor yet entirely what is done. Some, it is true, take ineffaceable impressions of character at once. Others dally, loiter, and get blown this way and that . . .
>
> There is also the highly respectable opinion that character-mongering is much overdone nowadays. . . .
>
> 'That young man, Jacob Flanders,' they would say, 'so distinguished looking – and yet so awkward.' Then they would apply themselves to Jacob and vacillate eternally between the two extremes.
>
> (*JR*, 150–1)

The narrator is positioned as a detective gathering 'hints', even the nature of which is mysterious ('not exactly . . . nor yet entirely'). 'Character-mongering' as the art of slotting people into fixed categories, is apparently denounced, but denounced in the language of the character-mongers themselves – 'the highly respectable opinion' – which also mocks those who debunk the society gossips, so that finally it is impossible to know where the narrator stands.

In fact, the questions as to Jacob's categorization bring into view the necessity of casting any biographical subject into typical moulds organized around standard pairs of oppositional terms, such as 'awkward or distinguished looking', in order to give the subject recognizable 'characteristics'. This structure is also applied to what is alleged as a preliminary division between two mutually exclusive modes of formation. There is a distinction between those who are 'at once' printed or stamped with the 'ineffaceable impressions of character', and those who remain impressionable 'and get blown this way and that'. This is like the dilemma as to whether or not Orlando is someone whose character is fixed by the age of thirty (*O*, 152). In both cases, the fixed and the malleable, the character is moulded from the outside rather than having any identity to begin with: at every level of character-reading and character-formation, biographer and subject can only 'vacillate eternally between two extremes'. The vacillation is limited by its alternation between marked pairs and the poles of each pair are limited by being defined in terms of the opposite one.

The second way in which the biographical genre is undermined is related to this. It involves, on the one hand, a breaking up of the narrative so that there can be no illusion of smooth development, of one thing following another in a logical, predetermined line; and, on the other, a failure to give prominence to what are normally regarded as the chief turning points in a young man's progress.[2] But this, ironically, only draws attention to what is in fact the typical, normative structure of the great man's biography. A great man is given due weight or gravity by being shown to resemble, rather than to differ from, every other: his greatness is a function of his life's proceeding not exceptionally or idiosyncratically, but along well-known, recognizable lines.

Once again, it is the predicament of the old lady in the railway compartment which will show this more clearly. The following passage occurs immediately after the announcement, in a paragraph of a single sentence: 'Jacob

Flanders, therefore, went up to Cambridge in October, 1906' (27):

> 'This is not a smoking-carriage,' Mrs Norman protested, nervously but very feebly, as the door swung open and a powerfully built young man jumped in. He seemed not to hear her. The train did not stop before it reached Cambridge, and here she was shut up alone, in a railway carriage, with a young man.
>
> (*JR*, 27)

'Mrs Norman', it should first be said, has only entered the narrative in this paragraph. Woolf's narrators frequently give themselves this privilege of introducing transient characters by name and without further explanation: as if to get away from the 'man with a red moustache' and offer a title for the character's book, or to muddle the whole structural organization of differentiated character reading, in novels as on omnibuses or trains, so that the reader-of-the-narrator-as-reader is not provided with any consistent grasp on the position from which each person is viewed.

Then, the shift here to Mrs Norman follows the marking of one of the young man's major rites of passage ('Jacob Flanders, therefore, went up to Cambridge in October, 1906'). The narrator moves away from the hero and instead occupies the position of a stranger (to him) whom he happens to come across in the train. Not only does this detract from the solemnity of the young man's progress, by transferring the focus of attention to someone else, but it also turns Jacob the possibly unique hero into a mere type as seen from the place of Mrs Norman.

The typing, further, casts or moulds him as nothing more or less than a potentially threatening 'powerfully built' male. Having immediately jumped to her conclusions as to the possible sequence of events, given their solitariness and the difference of sex, Mrs Norman then takes precautionary measures:

> She touched the spring of her dressing-case, and ascertained that the scent-bottle and a novel from Mudie's were both handy (the young man was standing

> up with his back to her; putting his bag in the rack). She would throw the scent-bottle with her right hand, she decided, and tug the communication cord with her left. She was fifty years of age, and had a son at college. Nevertheless, it is a fact that men are dangerous.
>
> (*JR*, 27)

'This is not a smoking-carriage' is thus reinterpreted as being the socially acceptable translation of an unspeakable premise, the 'fact that men are dangerous', into the mildness of 'All men smoke', the inconvenience of the latter practice being a legitimate cause for polite protest.

Mrs Norman both refers herself to, and attempts to avert the acting out of, a representative or likely story of what may happen to women left alone in railway carriages with men. At the same time, she sees the potential for another story, which makes her old enough to be his mother and therefore makes him like her own son rather than like one of the 'men' of whom women are justifiably afraid. It is this second, conflicting story which eventually gains the upper hand:

> But since, even at her age, she noted his indifference, presumably he was in some way or other – to her at least – nice, handsome, interesting, distinguished, well built, like her own boy? One must do the best one can with her report. Anyhow, this was Jacob Flanders, aged nineteen. It is no use trying to sum people up. One must follow hints, not exactly what is said, nor yet entirely what is done.
>
> (*JR*, 28)

It is striking that the last two sentences anticipate verbatim the passage already quoted, towards the end of the novel:

> How far was Jacob Flanders at the age of twenty-six a stupid fellow? It is no use trying to sum people up. One must follow hints, not exactly what is said, nor yet entirely what is done.
>
> (*JR*, 150)

In the second occurrence, the sentiments are attributed to the narrator rather than to any Mrs Norman, which then reinforces retrospectively the impression from the first passage that Mrs Norman has herself become a figure for the narrator – who, further on, marks this by noting her similar difference of age and sex from the object of her investigation. But the second passage also makes the narrator 'one' with Mrs Norman, the old lady in the railway carriage.

The shift from seeing Jacob in the train as a man (and dangerous) to seeing him as like a son (and safe) might be read as a move which turns him, in the eyes of the woman, from a type to an individual, and from a stranger to an intimately known friend. But the 'hints' which Mrs Norman follows, and the conclusions she draws, are no nearer to any 'Jacob' when she is likening him to her son than when she is taking him as belonging to the class of men. The process occurs through an ordered examination of the evidence:

> She read half a column of her newspaper; then stealthily looked over the edge to decide the question of safety by the infallible test of appearance . . .
>
> . . . Taking note of socks (loose), of tie (shabby), she once more reached his face. . . . All was firm, yet youthful, indifferent, unconscious – as for knocking one down! No, no, no! . . .
>
> Nobody sees anybody as he is, let alone an elderly lady sitting opposite a strange young man in a railway carriage. They see a whole – they see all sorts of things – they see themselves. . . . Should she say to the young man (and after all he was just the same age as her own boy): 'If you want to smoke, don't mind me'?
>
> (*JR*, 27–8; first ellipsis in text)

With the change in the reading of his features – from 'powerfully built' (27) to 'nice, handsome, interesting, distinguished, well built, like her own boy' (28) goes a shift not from class to individual but from one class to another. The two are mutually exclusive and structurally related, so that the reassignment of Jacob to the second necessitates a vehement repudiation of the initial interpretation ('No, no, no!'). The statement that 'nobody sees anybody as he is' follows the revised interpretation, implying the inadequacy of either of the two mutually defining categories. Both for men and for sons, there is a well-established lexicon of appropriate adjectives.

The act of judging by conventional signs, 'the infallible test of appearance', is taken to caricatural lengths here – the evidence of, and the appropriate classifications for, socks and ties – with Mrs Norman becoming something like a would-be detective. But again, this only complicates the issue in the light of the overlap between her and the narrator. The narrator's typing of Mrs Norman as 'an elderly lady sitting opposite a strange young man in a railway carriage', and hence all the less able to 'see anybody as he really is' applies equally to herself, another detective or would-be disinterested realist who can only 'follow hints' and fail to 'sum people up'.

With the scene in the railway carriage, then, Woolf tells the typical story of a middle-aged woman's telling of typical stories faced with an unknown man. He can only be read with equanimity by being transferred from the class of men to the class of family members: he is first regarded as savage and then domesticated to the familiarity of every mother's son. But she also shows that there is no reading of character outside the type. The public scene presents women with its unknown faces and potential dangers to be read and reread according to a prescribed sequence, so that the alien and fearful may be accommodated and the railway compartment become just like home. But this structure is itself what produces the illusion of depth and individuality in the contrasted figures of the family: as before, the standard model of the type generates the exceptional status and uniqueness of those who are supposed to be something more.

It is not, then, a question of reading behind or beyond the conventional signs and typifications to understand a genuine as opposed to a superficial story or the complete book of each character as opposed to a few hints or fragments. Rather, what Woolf suggests is that it is not possible to separate conventional signs, characters, stories and the reality which they structure and interpret.

In *Mrs Dalloway*, this construction of typical stories is itself theorized as a phenomenon with typical biographical stages:

> Clarissa once, going on top of an omnibus with him somewhere, Clarissa superficially at least, so easily

> moved, now in despair, now in the best of spirits, all aquiver in those days and such good company, spotting queer little scenes, names, people from the top of a bus, for they used to explore London and bring back bags full of treasures from the Caledonian market – Clarissa had a theory in those days – they had heaps of theories, always theories, as young people have. It was to explain the feeling they had of dissatisfaction; not knowing people; not being known. For how could they know each other? (*MD*, 135)

'So easily moved' suggests the 'susceptibility' Peter Walsh has just noted in himself, and which likens him to the Clarissa to whom he returns as both intimate companion and stranger: they share the making of stories and theories of 'scenes, names, people', but this is explained as a need to explain their lack of knowledge of each other as well. Further, Peter casts their youthful complicity into the mould of the typical: 'outside passenger' (*JR*, 62) now to his own past, he sees himself and Clarissa then as having theories 'as young people have', as if the theory he holds has moved from one of absolute individuality (people don't know each other) to one of types (young people's having theories about people is to be explained by their youth). Theory-making has been simplified and stratified into typical categories, including the category of youth as a time of theory-making, now supposedly surpassed: Clarissa and his youthful self can now be classified in the shorthand terms of the type, like 'the man with the red moustache' (*JR*, 62).

The opening omnibus quotation gives an urban setting to its textual topography of the process of reading a past or a person;[3] and in *Jacob's Room* the questions of narrative perspective and character-reading are regularly understood as analogous to map-making:

> The streets of London have their map; but our passions are uncharted. What are you going to meet if you turn this corner?
>
> 'Holborn straight ahead of you,' says the policeman. Ah, but where are you going if instead of brushing past the old man with the white beard, the silver medal, and

> the cheap violin, you let him go on with his story, which ends in an invitation to step somewhere, to his room, presumably, off Queen's Square, and there he shows you a collection of birds' eggs and a letter from the Prince of Wales's secretary, and this (skipping the intermediate stages) brings you one winter's day to the Essex coast, where the little boat makes off to the ship, and the ship sails and you behold on the skyline the Azores, and the flamingoes rise; and there you sit on the verge of the marsh drinking rum-punch, an outcast from civilization, for you have committed a crime, are infected with yellow fever as likely as not, and – fill in the sketch as you like.
>
> As frequent as street corners in Holborn are these chasms in the continuity of our ways. Yet we keep straight on.
>
> (*JR*, 92–3)

The twists and turns here are numerous. The analogy of 'uncharted passions' to the street map becomes an actual walk, but a walk without a map (the policeman must be consulted). Then the decision not to proceed 'straight on' according to the official directions leads to the pause on the corner with the old man, the telling of whose story (otherwise ignored, unknown) transports 'you' to his room, to the coast and thence to exotic foreign parts, where the distinction between you and him as 'an outcast from civilization' is no longer clear.

This is also – as with the likely story of the old lady in the corner of the railway carriage – offered as a typical story (the probable yellow fever, the advice to 'fill in the sketch as you like'), which then raises the question of the ready-made map for understanding the stories of, for example, old men encountered on London street corners. The old man is both fitted into an existing plan, and, through the identification which has occurred by the end, assimilated to the reader of his story.[4]

If 'we keep straight on' despite such 'chasms in the continuity of our ways', that is also, then, because the chasms can be crossed or covered over (by the abolition of the difference with the other, by the making out of a story already mapped). This is similar to a structure described in Woolf's autobiographical 'Sketch of the Past':

> I find that scene making is my natural way of marking the past. Always a scene has arranged itself: representative; enduring. This confirms me in my instinctive notion: (it will not bear arguing about it; it is irrational) the sensation that we are sealed vessels afloat on what it is convenient to call reality; and at some moments, the sealing matter cracks; in floods reality; that is, these scenes – for why do they survive undamaged year after year unless they are made of something comparatively permanent? Is this liability to scenes the origin of my writing impulse? Are other people also scene makers? These are questions to which I have no answer. . . . Obviously I have developed the faculty, because, in all the writing I have done, I have almost always had to make a scene . . . when I am writing about a person; I must find a representative scene in their lives.
>
> (*MB*, 142–3)

What is striking here is that the 'reality' that 'floods' in on the barely watertight vessels is also 'representative, enduring' and 'arranged'. It is not an amorphous mass but a solid structure, or both at once; the scenes 'survive undamaged year after year' and are also in some way a permanent threat to the floating vessels. 'Reality' is both the medium in which the boats remain afloat, and what is always about to sink them.[5]

The 'representative scenes' both cause a 'crack' in the habitual sealing material of the floating selves and have a quality of monumental continuity. And this ambiguity could well be one of the characteristics of the work of art for Woolf: at once a chasm in the normal passage (urban and textual), and something which makes a connected narrative to cover over what would otherwise be exposed as the normality of that abyss, 'as frequent as street corners'. The old man's personal book is opened and read, to the point where he becomes one with the reader: the further the stranger is regarded as someone different, someone with a story, the more he is actually rendered indifferent, or other than unique, transferred himself to the reader who by the same movement takes on his identity.

The following passage could be taken as an account of the making of the typical upper-middle-class version of that surface 'reality':

> No doubt we should be, on the whole, much worse off than we are without our astonishing gift for illusion. At the age of twelve or so, having given up dolls and broken our steam engines, France, but much more probably Italy, and India almost for a certainty, draws the superfluous imagination. One's aunts have been to Rome; and every one has an uncle who was last heard of – poor man – in Rangoon. He will never come back any more. But it is the governesses who start the Greek myth. Look at that for a head (they say) – nose, you see, straight as a dart, curls, eyebrows – everything appropriate to manly beauty. . . . The point is, however, that we have been brought up in an illusion.
>
> (*JR*, 133)

The typical family mythology sketched out here slips into the language of its articulation, with the parenthetical 'poor man' imitating the way the common tragedy would be told to the child. The Greek heroic model could be linked to Woolf's stories of her mother's first husband; 'He must have been to her the perfect man; heroic; handsome; magnanimous; "the great Achilles, whom we knew" – it seems natural to quote Tennyson' (*MB*, 104). It suggests the way that she relates the formation of a 'character' to the finding of objects of desire via the stories that come its way. In the passage above, the fantasies which will drive the ex-train drivers and others are imbibed through the telling of tales of 'one's aunts', of the universal uncle, and on the part of one's governesses. Playing with dolls and trains hints at (but does not specify) a conventional differentiation according to sex; but by the end of the passage, 'the governesses' are inculcating into charges presumably of either sex a model of 'manly beauty'.

In this novel, the Greek ideal is ambiguously related to the possibility of Jacob's 'peculiar disposition – long rumoured among them' (150), and the undecidable identity of the sex to be educated in the beauties of the Greek male prepares the way for another minor scandal in the overtly female identification of the narrator. This is clear at the point where Jacob has just seen his Florinda 'upon another man's arm':

> Whether we know what was in his mind is another question. Granted ten years' seniority and a difference of sex, fear of him comes first; this is swallowed up by a desire to help – overwhelming sense, reason, and the time of night; anger would follow close on that – with Florinda, with destiny; and then up would bubble an irresponsible optimism. 'Surely there's enough light in the street at this moment to drown all our cares in gold!' Ah, what's the use of saying it? Even while you speak and look over your shoulder towards Shaftesbury Avenue, destiny is chipping a dent in him. He has turned to go. As for following him back to his rooms, – that we won't do.
>
> Yet that, of course, is precisely what one does.
>
> (*JR*, 91–92)

As before, the street scene as the model of the narrator's view is literal: she is first afraid of him, then there behind her Jacob, as if a replacement for the faithless girl or a sympathetic older sister. The question of what is in Jacob's mind becomes in the next sentence a series of responses to what might or might not be there on the part of the narrator, who has first stated the social determinants of her judgements (greater age and different sex). Like Mrs Norman, she constructs a likely story on the basis of her evidence.

The narrator poses as a potential source of consolation but also, and equally openly, shows her interest in seeing what happens, restraining and then giving way to the wish to continue as unseen observer of Jacob into the privacy of his rooms. Given that she identifies herself as of different sex, the passage also hints that this form of narrative exploration may be a specifically feminine enquiry into the nature of masculinity. (As with Mrs Norman, 'fear of him comes first', but is then superseded by other reactions.)

This operates also as an exposure of the conventions of what can now be identified as a masculine realism, by marking the actual presence on the scene of a narrator whose powers of omniscience then have to appear to be practically negotiated. The disconnections of the narrative from paragraph to paragraph, more blatant in *Jacob's Room* than in any of Woolf's other novels, map into the text this movement whereby there is neither a single perspective for the narrator taking an overview of a complete scene or subject or person, nor a smooth progression from one point to another in the object of her view. This could be seen as a feminine form of narrative: in breaking up the sequence of what would otherwise appear as a coherent and natural development, and in making this way of looking the different view of a woman. Woolf's 'travelling' shots make visible the place of the camera, which is not in a fixed position, and thereby also disturb the security of the identification of what is looked at. The novel of a young man's development is told from the point of view of the woman as outsider: outsider both to the institutionalized stages through which the youth passes, and to the conventions according to which they are represented as natural.

The outsider position is relevant in another way. For 'the difference of view', like 'the difference of value', is not simply a matter of two equal alternatives. If Woolf uses the casual example of football *v.* shopping in *A Room of One's Own* (70–1), pointing out that the match between them is fixed from the start by the privileging of the first, that hierarchy also comes into play, or rather into power, in the matter of ways of seeing. In *Jacob's Room* this comes to a head with a look at the citadels of masculine power. As with the vacuous Prime Minister of *Mrs Dalloway*, the prestige of men of power is effectively correlated not with a difference of talent or worth, but with the lack of any difference, here taken to its logical conclusion. Not only are they all the same, uniformly null, but they are machines, without any degree of individual agency.

Whitehall regularly figures in Woolf's writing as the bastion of 'that purely patriarchal society' of England (*ROO*, 71). It is taken in *Jacob's Room* to be the centre of a modern world of powerful, short-term communications, drawing into its network homogenized stories designed to 'cover' the world:[6]

> The wires of the Admiralty shivered with some far-away communication. A voice kept remarking that Prime

> Ministers and Viceroys spoke in the Reichstag; entered Lahore; said that the Emperor travelled; in Milan they rioted; said there were rumours in Vienna; said that the Ambassador at Constantinople had audience with the Sultan; the fleet was at Gibraltar. The voice continued, imprinting on the faces of the clerks in Whitehall . . . something of its own inexorable gravity, as they listened, deciphered, wrote down. Papers accumulated, inscribed with the utterances of Kaisers, the statistics of ricefields, the growling of hundreds of work-people, plotting sedition in back streets, or gathering in the Calcutta bazaars, or mustering their forces in the uplands of Albania, where the hills are sand-coloured, and bones lie unburied.
>
> (*JR*, 168)

It is an anonymous 'voice', like the one in *Between the Acts*, which is the source of all meaning, 'imprinting' the clerks' faces with a mechanical 'gravity' – depth and engraving – to make them, quite literally or to the letter, 'types' or 'characters'. Unlike the omnibus passengers, people here are not modelled on books with the potential for in-depth reading, but likened to mere surfaces on which transient daily information is marked. The bits of news are presented in random assortment, like the cuttings of a newspaper, one thing after another with no principle of unity. The passage continues:

> The voice spoke plainly in the square quiet room with heavy tables, where one elderly man made notes on the margin of type-written sheets, his silver-topped umbrella leaning against the bookcase.
>
> His head – bald, red-veined, hollow-looking – represented all the heads in the building. His head, with the amiable pale eyes, carried the burden of knowledge across the street; laid it before his colleagues, who came equally burdened; and then the sixteen gentlemen, lifting their pens or turning perhaps rather wearily in their chairs, decreed that the course of history should shape itself this way or that way, being manfully determined, as their faces showed, to impose some coherency upon

> Rajahs and Kaisers and the muttering in bazaars, the secret gatherings, plainly visible in Whitehall, of kilted peasants in Albanian uplands; to control the course of events.
>
> (*JR*, 168)

The imperative to 'impose some coherency' on the heterogeneity of what is ironically said to be 'plainly visible' in Whitehall reduces the rule of the world to a weary effort on the part of a 'hollow-looking' old man and his peers. The world comes to them in its already reported form; their task is simply to 'control the course' or arrange into the coherent form of a story what the 'wires' have already decreed to be 'events'.

In *The Waves*, Louis personifies the fantasy of complete mastery invoked here:

> I roll the dark before me, spreading commerce where before there was chaos in the far parts of the world. If I press on, from chaos making order, I shall find myself where Chatham stood, and Pitt, Burke and Sir Robert Peel.
>
> (*W*, 113)

'Manfully determined' retains that ambition, though in a less absolute form, and reveals its absurdity, for it marks the opposite of the actual situation of the officials. Rather than responsible agency, theirs is a mindless uniformity, measured as a thoroughly automated set of responses in the pyramidal structure from clerks to 'heads'. The men are just points in the network of communications which covers the world with the wires along which circulate selected pieces of information on matters to be construed as controllable events.

As in *Three Guineas*, Woolf's most extended 'outsider' view of the absurdity joined to the force of the masculine 'procession', satire is a principal strategy here:

> Pitt and Chatham, Burke and Gladstone looked from side to side with fixed marble eyes and an air of immortal quiescence which perhaps the living may have envied, the air being full of whistling and concussions, as the procession with its banners passed down Whitehall. Moreover, some were troubled with dyspepsia; one had

at that very moment cracked the glass of his spectacles; another spoke in Glasgow tomorrow; altogether they looked too red, fat, pale or lean, to be dealing, as the marble heads had dealt, with the course of history.

(*JR*, 168–9)

Louis's dreams – this time of being a future Pitt or Chatham – bite the dust again. In their mutually exclusive pairings, the four alternatives 'red, fat, pale or lean' leave, of course, no imaginable appearance for a face that might look fit to deal with 'the course of history': this is a matter for the marble. The 'air of immortal quiescence' redoubles the state of those who turn 'rather wearily in their seats', as if already dead. Between the illusion of a spectacle of great dead men still overlooking the scene and the reduction of the living in the narrator's eyes to a set of personal mishaps (broken glasses and bad digestion), there is no place left for the existence, past or present, of anything like an actual great man. Or rather, this makes of great men the ultimate in manufactured types. They are simulacra imprinted with the attributes of a bygone, never-more-to-be-attained solidity, making of authority no more than an inert imitation; and/or they are a collection of mildly grotesque fools.

'The course of history' controlled by great men then falls as a myth, the 'illusion' the living live by, as does the notion that once there were great men, great books and great events whereas now there are only mechanical people and a world of ephemera and fragments. But, as the governesses' stories indicate, there is no suggestion of doing without 'illusion', or without the potency of public and private stories. And by the same token, this arbitrary authority can only be exposed by a parallel move that mimics the same arbitrary homogenization, in exposing all the rulers as identical, and automatons. In order to show up the devices of ordering and typing, Woolf's narrator is obliged to engage in a kind of countertyping on the part of the outsider.

An alternative view, however, seems to posit some more authentic form of communication waiting to be released behind the wires and networks of the 'ruling lines' (38):

And the notes accumulate. And the telephones ring. And everywhere we go wires and tubes surround us to carry

> the voices that try to penetrate before the last card is dealt and the days are over. 'Try to penetrate,' for as we lift the cup, shake the hand, express the hope, something whispers, Is this all? Can I never know, share, be certain? Am I doomed all my days to write letters, send voices, which fall upon the tea-table, fade upon the passage, making appointments, while life dwindles, to come and dine?
>
> (*JR*, 90)

Up to this point, the passage assumes a given 'I' with a fixed term of life which cannot but be wasted, dwindle, as it vainly attempts to get through. There is a gap between 'us' and the 'wires and tubes' that carry the voices. 'Making appointments . . . to come and dine' wedges in with its social superficiality the unreachable 'life' which is thereby eaten away.

But then the narrator goes on: 'Yet letters are venerable; and the telephones valiant, for the journey is a lonely one, and if bound together by notes and telephones we went in company, perhaps – who knows? – we might talk by the way' (90). Here 'we' are not prior to the communications and conventional forms, but rather 'we' follow from, and are positioned as communicating individuals by, the 'notes and telephones', which are the condition of our possible talking 'by the way'. In the first model, 'I' is cut off from communication with others by the intervention of lines which can only diminish the fullness of personal expression. In the second, it is the lines which produce the structure in which 'we' are bound together 'in company', rather than cutting off the possibility of intimacy and cutting down the length of life. There is thus, once again, no individual self before the lines that make it recognize itself in relation to others: there is no book of individual character before the type.

But Woolf's narrators do not see these lines as neutral. If line and type there must be before the book of the self, the typical 'ruling lines' (38) of the 'manfully determined' (168) have been one-sided and one-way. To show the lines up as lines – the narrator on the scene, the spurious 'course of history', and the fantasy of male power – would be part of the process of changing their direction.

7 Things

> James Ramsay, sitting on the floor cutting out pictures from the illustrated catalogue of the Army and Navy Stores, endowed the picture of a refrigerator, as his mother spoke, with heavenly bliss.
>
> *TL*, 9

Near the beginning of her biography of Roger Fry, Woolf quotes part of a list compiled towards the end of her life by Fry's mother, who lived to the age of ninety-seven. This list consists of two categories: 'Things that were not – : Things that were: when I was a little child':

> Among the things that were not, she counted lucifer matches; hot-water bottles; night-lights; Christmas trees; hoardings with posters; Japanese anemones; spring mattresses; and gas for teeth extraction. Among the things that were, she counted flint and steel; rushlights; prunes and senna; clogs and pattens; beadles and chariots; tippets and sleeves (in one); snuff-boxes and Chartists.
>
> (*RF*, 17)

'She drew no conclusion,' adds Woolf, 'and it is left for us to infer that there were more denials than delights, more austerities than luxuries in the life of the little Quaker girl' (*RF*, 17). But this is not the only possible inference; indeed, the very starkness of the two sets of 'things' undecorated by adjectival hints casts doubt on the validity of any kind of inference. By the same token, it leaves the reader entirely free to construct different interpretations. Precisely because it offers 'no conclusion', Lady Fry's list is rich in suggestions for ways of thinking about the representation of historical change and the significance of 'things' in the construction of a biographical story.

Characters in Woolf's novels often mark their perceptions of the difference of the present from the period of their childhood by enumerating the objects that are new. One of the old ladies watching the Victorian episode in Miss La Trobe's play speculates on the difference of now from what is being represented as the ''Ome sweet 'Ome' of the nineteenth century:

> Change had to come, she said to herself, or there'd have been yards and yards of Papa's beard, of Mama's knitting. Nowadays her son-in-law was clean shaven. Her daughter had a refrigerator.
>
> (*BA*, 174)

Domestic appliances (gas, electricity, the telephone), more rapid forms of transport (the car, the 'motor bus'), different and more ephemeral forms of reading and entertainment figure in similar ways in this novel as conventional notation for pointing to social changes.[1] The decline in church attendance is attributed by the vicar to 'the motor bike, the motor bus and the movies' (75); Isa's lack of interest in the library's classical volumes is taken as symptomatic of a generation:

> What remedy was there for her at her age – the age of the century, thirty-nine – in books? For her generation the newspaper was a book; and as her father-in-law had dropped the *Times*, she took it and read.
>
> (*BA*, 19–20)

It would be easy to see in the marking and specifying of change in 'things' a passage or narrative of a 'modernization' characterized by increased mechanization, short-term satisfactions and speed. From the relative stability of old-fashioned objects and traditional, long-established customs – lengthy books, lengthy beards, houses rather than 'bungalows' – the world of the twentieth century has moved on, and has declined: there are no longer any fixed points of reference for personal and collective identity.

Another common way of referring to 'things' would lend support to this interpretation. 'We live in things', says old Mrs Swithin as she shows William Dodge the bed in which she was born and the two portaits that have hung in the house all her life (*BA*, 70). The things that remain signify the changelessness and continuity which the new objects or inventions throw out of order. In *The Years*, a set of objects – items of furniture and household things – recur in different places and at different times: for example, the account book with its picture of a sacred cow with which Eleanor Pargiter takes over the family housekeeping ('That solid object might survive them all' (*Y*, 72)), or the hall table with its claw-like appendages. Objects are thus set up against one another as 'permanent' or 'new' – as continuing, out of time, from time immemorial, or as abruptly making their entries onto the scene.

This initial dichotomy turns out to be more complicated, however, in that traditional objects only acquire their connotation of permanence by virtue of outlasting their contemporaries: by their isolation as representative, and by being set alongside those newer objects which show them up as 'old'. 'Now' and 'then' are juxtaposed, put in the same place, so as to make their distinction evident, to produce the effect of an absolute division between times. Lady Fry's two lists operate in a similar way, since the negative – 'Things that were not' – refers to the present of things that (now) are; while the positive – 'Things that were' – refers to things that are definitively of the past, and whose pastness is only established from the perspective of the present where they can be seen to be no more: it is their absence that makes them meaningful.

In *The Years*, the objects refound from the past tend to appear in unlikely places, moved from the original family house to the lodgings occupied by unmarried daughters in obscure parts of London. The effect of recognizing them, for friends or members of the family seeing them in a different setting, is doubly strange. They stand as parts for whole, for the family domestic environment from which they have been separated, and also for the time remembered as a long-forgotten and buried past of childhood, but now abruptly, and partially, returned.

Two different ways of thinking about Woolf's concentration on the objects of everyday life might be considered, the first of which is the literary equivalent of the documentary history model to be considered in relation to *Orlando*.[2] Her attention to such details of décor would here be aligned with an 'objective' realism, supplying 'the whole picture' with 'photographic' exactitude, much as a BBC Classic or a Masterpiece Theater production makes sure of the historical accuracy of all the props. The accumulation of precise information about the social milieu could be linked with Woolf's interest in the minutiae of ordinary people's lives and experiences and in recording them for posterity. The proliferation of names for things, adding up to the impression of a 'material' world stuffed with clear-cut, identifiable objects, people and events, would go against any interpretation of her writing as formally experimental or working with language in an innovative mode.

It is this possibility which a second probable interpretation would develop. In this light, Woolf's fascination with isolated objects and the bric-à-brac of particular historical periods could be seen as entirely compatible with a modernist writing practice. World and objects hang loose, in no fixed relation either to one another or to a stable order of meaning: the 'whole' world of which the objects are parts, or the linguistic order where each word has its allotted place.

The line indicated above, that Woolf's novels point to the transition from a coherent, traditional world, where things and words are known and in their place, to a constantly changing world where everything is short-lived, mechanical and new, would be a kind of amalgam of both these positions. Such a view might aim to offer a narrative of the representational shift from realism to modernism, a move enacted by the forms of Woolf's own novels. Within individual novels, be they broadly 'realist' or 'modernist' in form, Woolf's explorations and teasings apart of historical and biographical narrative could be seen to repeat this paradigmatic move from a fundamental coherence to a fundamental disorder or instability where things and words fall apart – and sometimes to regain or to reassert that order.

But the opposition of realism and modernism is not so simple, even when 'realism' is reduced to the caricatural form in which Woolf castigates the Edwardian novelists in 'Mr Bennett and Mrs Brown'. What kind of representation, for instance, is Lady Fry's twofold list? Nothing, on the face of it, could be more straightforward than a pure enumeration of 'things', in which 'the facts speak for themselves' and no rhetorical ornamentation detracts from the clarity of names naming the objects to which they refer. On the other hand, nothing could be more peculiar or more apparently arbitrary: what is the relation *between* the words, the form of the connection? Lady Fry's list ought to be a perfect illustration of referential language reflecting the totality of things, each with their allotted name. But the oddness of 'the bare essentials' here has the unexpected effect of indicating instead the inadequacy of such a conception of the relation of words and things: a sequence of nouns is meaningless without further syntactic explanation. Named things are not primary, but get their meaning from the whole linguistic structure within which they are picked out.

To put this another way, we could consider the strange position of 'Chartists' shoulder to shoulder with all the snuff-boxes and sleeves. They seem to threaten the peaceful domesticity of senna and tippets (whatever they were), throwing in an ingredient from a completely different sphere of reference as if to prepare the ground for a posthumous novel by Sir Walter Scott. But this is only to show up the necessarily eccentric operation involved in any description of a given scene or world. 'Things' are identified as such only by their insertion into a representational context which gives a shared framework to their heterogeneity. This common sense makes them all recognizable, likening them in so far as they are 'things', and distinguishing them in so far as they have their own names. Lady Fry's eccentricity in not observing the rules of different orders of 'things' serves to show up the more pervasive eccentricity of 'common-sense' classifications in their necessary arbitrariness.

In *Orlando*, the 'object' version of history finds its ultimate form in the various catalogues of things introduced at different points: the inventory of items ordered for Orlando's refurbishing of her house some time after the Restoration (*O*, 68); the shopping list in the present ('boy's boots, bath salts, sardines' (187)) or the goods in nineteenth-century shops ('vast windows piled high with handbags and mirrors, and dressing gowns, and flowers, and fishing rods, and luncheon baskets' (172)), or the debris of Victoriana piled up in St James's Park:

> The most heterogeneous and ill-assorted objects, piled higgledy-piggledy in a vast mound where the statue of Queen Victoria now stands! Draped about a vast cross of fretted and floriated gold were widow's weeds and bridal veils; hooked on to other excrescences were crystal palaces, bassinettes, military helmets, memorial wreaths, trousers, whiskers, wedding cakes, cannon, Christmas trees, telescopes, extinct monsters, globes, maps, elephants, and mathematical instruments – the whole supported like a gigantic coat of arms on the right side by a female figure clothed in flowing white; on the left by a portly gentleman wearing a frock-coat and sponge-bag trousers.
>
> (*O*, 145)

The obscenity of these 'excrescences' (Orlando calls it a 'garish erection' (145)) seems to derive in part from the fact that what looks like a rubbish tip should actually be 'calculated to last for ever' (145). This literal pile-up of 'heterogeneous, ill-assorted objects' has the effect of exposing the relative absurdity of its textual equivalent in the listing of objects somehow supposed to add up to the 'portrait' of an age.

What is so striking about Lady Fry's lists (and Woolf tantalizingly only quotes a selection from them) is the absence of any syntactical or narrative link, either between the two categories or between the various 'things'. 'She drew no conclusion', indeed, leaving suspended the question of what, if anything, would account for the difference between the two. According to a well-known early essay by Roland Barthes, realist narratives seek to make connections between temporally separated events by the device of *post hoc, ergo propter hoc*, with what comes later in time appearing, through the tricks of narrative, to be caused or determined by what comes before.[3] In ignoring such codes, Lady Fry's inventory could thus be seen as a modernist 'degree zero' of the 'before and after' structure of any narrative: this, then this; things that were, things that were not. It works as an exposure of the construction of causality, since clearly the things which stand out as those which 'were' acquire their pastness only from the perspective of the second moment. The list could also be regarded as an ironic undermining of the biography of her more celebrated son into which it is inserted: the mother's 'unstory' or 'ur-story' gives a different aspect to the attempt to build up a coherent narrative in the case of Roger's life, in the same way that *Jacob's Room* is in part an undermining from the woman's point of view of the narrative of masculine development.

Just as Lady Fry's 'things' can be read in two opposite ways – as the limit point of either a realist or an anti-realist narrative – so the place of the 'things' in Woolf's novels can be seen as something other than either description – the backdrop of history – or, for example, figures for the autonomy of art as a 'thing' in itself. Nor, as we shall see in *Orlando*, can Woolf's representation of things be fitted in to what in itself would constitute a straightforwardly realistic narrative of the shift from stable orders of integration between people and things to the fragmentariness of modernity. Rather, this hypothetical shift – for individual subjects as for social groups, in terms of the construction of both biography and history – furnishes Woolf's novels with the stuff of which further questions will be made.

An interesting passage of *The Years* will serve to develop this. In the 'Present Day' section at the end, Peggy is with her old Aunt Eleanor. Eleanor comes up with a disconnected list not unlike Lady Fry's 'Things that were not':

> 'Yes – I don't know about aeroplanes, I've never been up in one: but motor cars – I could do without motor cars. I was almost knocked down by one, did I tell you? In the

> Brompton Road. All my own fault – I wasn't looking. . . . And wireless – that's a nuisance – the people downstairs turn it on after breakfast; but on the other hand – hot water; elecric light; and those new – ' She paused.
>
> (*Y*, 252)

Eleanor's enumeration of new things – 'those new – ' could all be placed under the heading of communications – forms of transport, media, or domestic conveniences. They thus lend themselves to that version of history which sees its mechanical inventions as indicating either progress – the improvement of the quality of life for all – or a general decline in that quality owing to the same mechanization, which would now signify a loss of authenticity, a speeding up of life and a trivialization or alienation of a previously more complete form of experience.

Peggy would seem to fall in with a version of the second of these views. After Eleanor has described some of her childhood to her, she prompts her aunt for more: 'She wished to get her back to her past. It was so interesting, so safe; so unreal – that past of the eighties; and to her, so beautiful in its unreality' (*Y*, 254). Already the attraction of that 'past' understood as 'safe' is associated with its 'unreality' as if it is automatically a fictional construction, an illusion of secure wholeness. In keeping with this, Peggy elaborates a story about her aunt as a type or representative of nineteenth-century certainties:

> It would be simple, she thought, it would be satisfactory, she thought . . . to be like that. . . .
>
> 'Take my aunt,' she said to herself, beginning to arrange the scene into an argument she had been having with a man at the hospital, 'take my aunt, living alone in a sort of workman's flat at the top of six flights of stairs . . .'
>
> . . . It was as if she still believed with passion – she, old Eleanor – in the things that man had destroyed. A wonderful generation, she thought, as they drove off. Believers . . .
>
> (*Y*, 253)

This vignette, first a consciously fabricated story to be recounted to a colleague, gathers coherence as an accurate report: 'The scene in the flat composed itself in Peggy's mind as she would tell it. . . . She glanced at Eleanor to verify the details' (253). Moving from composition to verification, again she looks at her 'as if to collect another little fact to add to her portrait of a Victorian spinster' (255). But the portrait disintegrates:

> She's not like that – not like that at all, she said, making a little dash with her hand as if to rub out an outline that she had drawn wrongly. . . .
>
> . . . Where does she begin, and where do I end? she thought . . . On they drove. They were two living people, driving across London; two sparks of life enclosed in two separate bodies; and those sparks of life enclosed in two separate bodies are at this moment, she thought, driving past a picture palace. But what is this moment and what are we? The puzzle was too difficult for her to solve it.
>
> (*Y*, 255)

The 'puzzle' is finding a language to represent Eleanor neither as the objectified typical 'Victorian spinster' stereotyped in a factual 'portrait', nor as an isolated metaphysical 'spark of life', cut off from any relationship to her milieu. The references to the car and the cinema focus the 'puzzle' in terms of a relation to moving images, seen from the car or on the screen. The view of the picture palace occurs as part of what is itself already a sequence of images seen from the car, and so extends the hall of screens and windows which might be seen to characterize modern life as a spectacle perpetually in motion, without a firm point of rest or origin. But the passage makes explicit the *interest* for Eleanor, from her perspective, in seeing in her aunt a representative of the safety and stability of a bygone period from which she takes the present time, and the form of her own relationship to her time, to have departed.

Woolf's narrative of the passage just prior to this one takes a different line, by focusing on one of 'those new' objects of domestic life: the telephone. North, a cousin returned from some years of farming in Africa,[4] is dining in a different London flat with Sara, and they are interrupted:

> 'I'm North,' he answered the telephone. 'I'm dining with Sara. . . . Yes, I'll tell her. . . . 'He looked at her again.

> 'She is sitting on the edge of her chair,' he said, 'with a smudge on her face, swinging her foot up and down.'
>
> Eleanor stood holding the telephone. She smiled, and for a moment after she had put the receiver back stood there, still smiling, before she turned to her niece Peggy, who had been dining with her.
>
> 'North is dining with Sara,' she said, smiling at the little telephone picture of two people at the other end of London . . .
>
> . . . But her niece did not smile, for she had not seen the picture, and she was slightly irritated because, in the middle of what they were saying, Eleanor [had] suddenly got up and said, 'I'll just remind Sara.' . . . While Eleanor telephoned, she had been looking at the picture of her grandmother over the writing-table.
>
> (*Y*, 247–8)

In both places, the telephone breaks in upon what had been a conversation between two people: at the calling end, Eleanor's decision to phone 'in the middle of what they were sayng'; at the receiving end, 'extreme irritation' (247) on Sara's part at the sound of the bell. But at the same time, the phone connects two of the four people and the link thus established between the two rooms is transferred on to the narrative line, as the scene shifts from Sara's to Eleanor's flat via the telephone call. The physical 'room' is no longer identifiable as a separate scene.

The possibility of a 'telephone picture' (248) represents in a new or different way the connection or difference between what Peggy calls 'two sparks of life', as the sound is translated into a recognizable image. ('One of these days, d'you think you'll be able to see things at the end of the telephone?' (250)). It is as though the separation of sight and sound which the telephone actualizes makes explicit the structure that operates in any attempt at making connections between what are thought to be two separate, self-contained 'people' ('Where does she begin, and where do I end?').

The objectivity of Peggy's hypothetical 'portrait' of a Victorian type is undermined further in the contrast between the 'telephone picture' and the picture of Eleanor's mother. This is one of the objects that recur in different places and at different times through *The Years* as ambivalent signs of the questions of continuity and change. Here, 'a flower fallen on the glass' (248) appears as a mutation in the image, at once a sign of time passing and a new event, as if the picture has a life of its own, a story that develops. But the dropped flower, it turns out, was there all the time: '"It was hidden by the dirt," said Eleanor. "But I can just remember it, when I was a child. That reminds me, if you want a good man to clean pictures – "' (248). The picture which might have been taken to symbolize a permanence or stability opposed to the ephemerality and arbitrariness of the modern 'telephone picture' thus has a complicated temporality of its own. The fallen flower is both there and not there all along; it is only seen to have been there when the picture is cleaned. In a similar way, the disjunction in representation suggested by the phone's separation of picture and voice may not indicate something radically new in the forms of subjectivity, but instead show up disjunctions and uncertainties that were there all the time, unobserved.

The telephone's interruption is also a figure for the impossibility, in Woolf, of positing the radical separation of one individual from another, or the autonomy of one consciousness to itself. As in *Mrs Dalloway*, characters are frequently split between at least two times or two places, and always questioning their ability to know one another or themselves ('What's "I"?' (108)). The 'moments' in Woolf when everything seems to come together – in a character's consciousness, in the achievement of a work of art, in communion between two people, in the integration of past with present time – stand out not as the culmination which makes a whole of the parts, or which reaches the end of the narrative line, but precisely as 'momentary' semblances of ending and completion or of origin, retrospectively glimpsed.

Lady Fry's lists, proposing neither a bygone unity nor an internal unity within either time, demonstrate the disorder which narratives of psychic or historical change have to try to cover over. *Orlando*, as the next chapter will show, is Woolf's most thorough exposure, by parody, of the narrative conventions which perform this 'sealing' process.[5]

8 Orlando's Undoing

> A man who can destroy illusions is both beast and flood. Illusions are to the soul what atmosphere is to the earth. Roll up that tender air and the plant dies, the colour fades. The earth we walk on is a parched cinder. It is marl we tread and fiery cobbles scorch our feet. By the truth we are undone. Life is a dream. 'Tis waking that kills us. He who robs us of our dreams robs us of life – (and so on for six pages if you will, but the style is tedious and may well be dropped).
>
> (*O*, 127)

More than any of Woolf's novels, *Orlando* destroys illusions – about history and biography and not least about 'a man' – or it might be a woman – 'who can destroy illusions'. For this passage is offered not straight but as a series of clichés: the idea of the destroyer of illusions is already *passé*. Where even parody is parodied, footholds for the reader are in short supply; so, a fortiori, are the points of reference that might ground a coherence relating to history and to human identity in a secure narrative style. *Orlando* leaves nothing (and not even 'nothing', the ultimate illusion of 'all is illusion') in place, or indeed in time.

In its narrative run-through of a series of distinct historical periods – from the Elizabethan sixteenth century to the 'present moment' in 1928 – the novel follows a pattern common to several of Woolf's works.[1] In this case, taking the ostensible hero(ine) of the biography to be a character who lives for five hundred years is a device first of all to show up the illusory position of the history-writer as a reliable reconstructor of a past 'world'. The fact that, within the terms of the fiction, Orlando does experience at first hand each successive age, and hence has the authority to compare them, exposes the dubious claims of the historian to 'know' a period other than his own.

This device is all the more effective from the fact that *Orlando* is written not as autobiography but as biography, introducing the further complication of the status of the recorder of Orlando's experiences. By thus foregrounding the position of the biographer as observer of the subject, Woolf is able to draw out many of the tricks of narrative by which his position is conventionally elided or effaced. He is supposed to reconstruct a balanced view of a 'life', much as a historian is supposed to reconstruct a neutral and accurate 'portrait' of an age.

There is thus a double undercutting of what can be called the 'life and times' mode of biography. *Orlando* looks at the ways in which history makes use of fictional codes of narration, and at how both history and biography imply particular conceptions of the relations between subjectivity and history – what 'makes' the man (or woman) or period that is represented as a discrete and describable entity.

In its abrupt passages from the sixteenth to the eighteenth century, and then, via the Victorian age, to the 'present moment', Woolf's narrative puts side by side two conventional conceptions of the criteria by which an 'age' may legitimately be identified. The first is broadly metaphysical and itself a clichéd formula – 'the spirit of the age':

> The transaction between a writer and the spirit of the age is one of infinite delicacy, and upon a nice arrangement between the two the whole fortune of his work depends. (*O*, 167)

The eighteenth century, for instance, is known as The Age of Enlightenment, or The Age of Reason – blanket terms which are supposed to cover what has been determined to be the outstanding characteristic of the given period. In this particular century, so the story goes, superstitions were swept away by philosophy (some general cultural mind being the prime moving force), and in conformity with this spirit, houses were built, music was composed and lives were lived according to newly rational principles. The Augustan age would be contrasted with the religious obfuscation or puritanical moralism which preceded it; and with the nineteenth-century utilitarianism (engendering industrialization and the Age of Progress) which succeeded it.

Such stories of the *Zeitgeist* are habitually progressive: they imply that the present, or some hypothetically projected future, is the end or telos to which previous ages have been tending, and to which they were or are only stepping stones on the way to arrival at a fully conclusive destination where Ages cease in the utopia of a timeless and placeless state of happiness. It is not accidental that the 'Enlightenment' spirit comes to mind as the first example, since this was the very period in which the paradigm of such *Zeitgeist* teleological histories was established. The mirror image of the metaphor of progressive enlightenment is a narrative of historical decline, leading ultimately to the darkness of apocalypse and harking back to a 'golden age' bathed in the sweetness and light of which the present age is now seen to stand in need.

In *Orlando*, the negative – pessimistic, nostalgic – version of the 'spirit of the age' form of history is offered by the dubious 'man of letters', Nick Greene, who in the sixteenth century mourns the non-equivalence of his age to that of the Greeks and in the nineteenth century bemoans the loss of the same (or different – now past) sixteenth century he once (at the time) deplored. In the first version the past, like the present, is a stage on the way to what the future will assuredly deliver; in the second, the past figures irrevocably as 'what has been lost'.

The second conventional model of a historical period utilized by *Orlando* is that of objective description, as in the claims of what was called 'photographic realism' in literature.[2] In this conception, historical periods would appear as a series of (accurately drawn) backdrops, like those of a play, constituting the milieu or environment against which the actors perform their more or less determined, pre-scripted parts. This was the model to which Lady Fry's minimal lists of 'things' seemed to make appeal. Verisimilitude is assumed by the specification of the objects which furnish the surroundings; differences between one age and another are established by pointing out new, or characteristic, everyday things, the 'props' of ordinary life.

The two poles of historical description – by things or by the spirit, object or subject, have in common an implied narrative about the progress or decline from one age to the next. Rarely does either imply or lay out a succession of separate and equal periods, though this might be expected of the 'backcloth' documentary narration which marks its difference from the evaluative stance of the *Zeitgeist* focus on the moral coherence of an age. The history-by-objects can, as the Victorian heaping of 'excrescences' cited in chapter 7 shows (*O*, 145), be a history of deterioration; it can also be one of progress, drawing close here to the model of gradual enlightenment, in which the appearance or invention of new objects is taken as a sign of the improvement of standards of living – of the 'conditions' of life. If the basic narrative is via externals – what Woolf habitually calls 'material' things – the mental or moral changes can be cited as extra or supplementary changes conditioned by the first. Reciprocally, if thought is taken to be the primary instance, the world in which it takes form will be said to follow suit. It is the difference between pointing out that the age of reason produced a more regular planned style of city architecture, and that the planning of symmetrically ordered cities and buildings in the eighteenth century was one of the environmental factors that induced a more logical, functional state of mind in its citizens.

This is Orlando poised in London at the end of the eighteenth century:

> Here and there, on one of the hills which rose above London was a stark gallows tree, with a corpse nailed to rot or parch on its cross; for danger and insecurity, lust and violence, poetry and filth swarmed over the tortuous Elizabethan highways and buzzed and stank – Orlando could remember even now the smell of them on a hot night – in the little rooms and narrow pathways of the

> city. Now – she leant out of her window – all was light, order, and serenity.
>
> (*O*, 140)

Until, that is, something else changes as she looks and listens to the chimes of St Paul's:

> With the twelfth stroke of midnight, the darkness was complete. A turbulent welter of cloud covered the city. All was darkness; all was doubt; all was confusion. The Eighteenth century was over; the Nineteenth century had begun.
>
> (*O*, 141)

This passage of three ages undermines several conventions of *Zeitgeist* history-writing. The mock specification of each period with a few representative abstract nouns highlights the problem of how the historian gets from one periodized compartment to another – here from the age of filth, etc., to light, to darkness – or (more cyclically reparaphrased), from confusion to order to confusion once again. And the status of the abstract is also muddled. 'Light, order and serenity' are represented as if they might literally be visible to a contemporary spectator, and this effect is then strengthened by the plunge of the semi-metaphorical light to the unequivocally palpable darkness of the cloud cover. By shifting the (metaphorical and literal) perspective in this way, a complicity is exposed between the apparently literal and the apparently metaphorical; and the passage achieves the same effect by mixing the registers of the nouns placed alongside each other. Those characterizing the first period – 'danger and insecurity, lust and violence, poetry and filth' – are patently heterogeneous; and the buzzing and stinking attributed for example to 'poetry' or 'insecurity' jar in the same way as the literalization of the *Zeitgeist* in a later passage: 'One might see the spirit of the age blowing, now hot, now cold, upon her cheeks' (147). In their juxtaposition, both literal and metaphorical, objective and abstract uses lose their separate credibility, because the illusion of a consistent 'picture' has been broken. Again, the conflation of things and ideas: 'The age was the Elizabethan; their morals were not ours; nor their poets; nor their climate; nor their vegetables even' (17). In citing the particulars which characterize a given period, the narrative finds itself immediately embroiled in a question of language: the type of words chosen to represent typical phenomena reveal themselves as metaphorical and interpretative, and all the more patently by confusing the boundaries of things and ideas: by literalizing the 'light' and 'dark' of an age as supposedly evidenced by an eye-witness report.

Orlando, then, unpicks both the language and the narrative codes of the forms of history-writing. To the extent that it posits the unity and internal coherence of distinct epochs it is unable to account for the passage from one to the other, and has to resort to a simple declaration of the break: one moment one age, one moment the next. The unity of each age further turns out to be not autonomous, but based on oppositions with those that precede and succeed it: the 'enlightenment' of the eighteenth century is only understood as such in relation to the 'darkness' which follows it.

These presuppositions of historical narrative show up in related ways for the writing of biography. Just as the historian is modelled on the impartial recorder or observer of relevant facts, so the biographer is supposed to be in the same position with regard to the 'life' of an individual. *Orlando* draws attention throughout to the selection, partiality and narrative devices which such an undertaking must presuppose, but generally obscures. First, there is the pretence of completeness and objectivity. *Orlando* regularly refers to 'documents' authenticating the account of the subject's doings, though in the general course of the narrative the biographer is actually situated as an 'omniscient' narrator, fully aware of the innermost thoughts of Orlando. The model of external objectivity, based on that of historical evidence, is openly parodied in the Constantinople section when allegedly only 'tantalizing fragments' (79), in the form of an English naval officer's diary and a letter from a young English woman to 'a female friend in Tunbridge Wells' (80), remain to give an account of the fire which takes place during Orlando's investiture as a duke.

In her own venture into 'real' biography, *Roger Fry*, Woolf was as self-effacing as the fictional biographer of Orlando is not: rarely does Fry's narrator announce or expatiate upon her own interest in the composition of this 'life'. So much so that one of the few and most illuminating hints in this direction is made with reference not to her writing on Fry but to Fry's on Paul Cézanne: 'Never does he draw attention by irrelevance or display to his own share in the work of reconstruction' (*RF*, 285). It is as if the very declaration of modesty must be distanced from the biographer who must not reveal herself as such, for fear of threatening the structure by which the illusion is built.

Orlando's biographer is always thrusting him- or herself into the story to point out, and thereby destroy, the devices generally used to secure the illusions of coherence and causal sequence. Before the heralded 'event' which turns out to be the birth of Orlando's child in the twentieth century, the biographer takes the reader off on a tour of Kew Gardens, having distracted her with a sound:

> Is nothing then, going to happen this pale March morning to mitigate, to veil, to cover, to conceal, to shroud this undeniable event whatever it may be? For after giving that sudden, violent start, Orlando – but Heaven be praised, at this very moment there struck up outside one of these frail, reedy, fluty, jerky, old-fashioned barrel-organs which are still sometimes played by Italian organ-grinders in back streets. Let us accept the intervention, humble though it is, as if it were the music of the spheres, and allow it, with all its gasps and groans, to fill this page with sound until the moment comes when it is impossible to deny its coming; which the footman has seen coming and the maid-servant; and the reader will have to see too . . .
>
> (*O*, 183)

and so follow a couple of pages of mock pastoral culminating in the announcement of the happy and unexpected event. At one and the same time, this passage exposes both the teleological construction of biographical narrative (its positing of significant, climactic moments or events) and the pretence at covering every moment: the biographer has to distract the reader for the exact time it will take before the crucial moment is reached.[3]

'Is nothing then going to happen?' might be taken as emblematic of the task of making sure that something does appear to happen, that the life can be marked and structured by the recording of significant events. The other, contradictory side of this predicament is brought out by the possibility of precisely such 'dead time':

> It was now November. After November, comes December. Then January, February, March, and April. After April comes May. June, July, August follow. Next is September. Then October, and so, behold, here we are back at November again, with a whole year accomplished.
>
> This method of writing biography . . . is a little bare, perhaps, and the reader, if we go on with it, may complain that he could recite the calendar for himself and so save his pocket whatever sum the Hogarth Press may think proper to charge for this book.
>
> (*O*, 167)

The selection of what will count as a significant event in the 'life' is paralleled by the acknowledgement that hypothetical completeness, apart from entailing an interminable story, would be undifferentiated to the point of being meaningless. The illusion that one month, or one hour, stands out from others, is indispensable to the making or 'reconstruction' of a life-story. The reference to the Hogarth Press then points up the institutional expectations associated with the genre of biography – but if one 'life' has to be more or less recognizable as conforming to the conventions of life-stories, then it turns out, ironically enough, as we saw with *Jacob's Room*, that resemblance is as much a criterion of its acceptability as the 'uniqueness' of the individual which a biography might seem to claim.

The Hogarth Press reference situates the biography as subject to publishing conventions of the marketable 'life'; and elsewhere Woolf uses linguistic rather than social indicators to demonstrate the complicity between biographical writing and fictional devices of selection and suspense. Half a page in parenthesis follows and expands upon the announcement that after Orlando's lawsuit decree finally came through, 'the whole town was filled with rejoicings' (159) – 'all of which', the narrator pursues, 'is properly enclosed in square brackets as above, for the good reason that a parenthesis it was without any importance in Orlando's life. She skipped it, to get on with the text' (160). Here, Orlando is positioned as the reader of her own, already written life – parodying the actual situation in which it is the biographer who decides what is relevant and what is not. Not only this: it is as if the irrelevant, parenthetical part is also present as part of the text – whereas in the supposed reality of the life to which it refers, this is precisely what Orlando 'skips', so that it is not part of her life at all. Further, the passage suggests by inversion the impossibility of making a radical separation betwen the life to be represented and the subsequent recording of it in narrative form: the subject is always in the process of writing, or reading, a 'life', the plausible boundaries of whose representation are prescribed in advance. It would thus be somewhat hasty to set up a distinction between the 'actual' life and the selection – or formal organization – of the biographical highlights; and this is a problem which is especially pertinent in the case of Woolf herself.

(Parenthetically, it is worth remarking in this context how often Woolf's critics and biographers seek to establish the extent to which her fictional plots and characters did or did not repeat or lightly modify experiences and persons from her 'own' life. It appears rather that Orlando's biographer (or Orlando him/herself) recognizes that conventions of biographical coherence operate continually in the process by which everyone is constantly constructing and censoring autobiographical stories about themselves: at a minimal level, fitting what are deemed significant events and turning points into a ready-made sequential and logical form. Nor is it enough to say that the diaries Woolf kept provided her with the 'raw material' for her novels, as though the record of a single day, for being less formally structured (which is anyway a *convention* of the private diary), more detailed, more fragmentary, were any the less a 'reconstruction' and selection than the novels themselves. This is to suppose that there is a prior, actual life or day to which the dashed-off diary is more faithful than the refined and formalized novel. But no evidence could be found for this original version other than in a textual form – which would then raise all the same problems. On the contrary, the 'raw material' claim could just as well be put the other way around, since the novels are always approaching a point at which the narrative illusion of the coherence of plots and characters over an extended period breaks down into the disconnections of heterogeneous pieces of dailiness: to find a literary form for the representation of daily life, or to put the whole of 'life' into a single day (*Mrs Dalloway*, *Between the Acts*) is exactly what Woolf attempts to achieve in her novels.)

A final example of *Orlando*'s exposure of the mechanisms of biographical narration is itself a parody of the middle section, 'Time Passes', of Woolf's own *To the Lighthouse*:

> Here he came then, day after day, week after week, month after month, year after year. He saw the beech trees turn golden and the young ferns unfurl; he saw the moon sickle and then circular; he saw – but probably the reader can imagine the passage which should follow . . . how things remain much as they are for two or three hundred years or so, except for a little dust and a few cobwebs which one old woman can sweep up in half an hour; a conclusion which, one cannot help feeling, might have been reached more quickly by the simple statement that 'Time passed' (here the exact amount could be indicated in brackets) and nothing whatever happened. (*O*, 61)

Most of this paragraph consists of a list of what it claims not to say ('probably, the reader can imagine'); 'the simple statement that "time passed"' has already been implicated by designating itself as such (and the same could be said of the parenthesis pointing out what a parenthesis might, but here does not, specify).

Any biography implies a theory of what constitutes the uniqueness or representativeness of its subject, and of individuals in general. To put the two most extreme alternatives: either individuals are wholly determined by their milieu, be this defined as material or spiritual, or they are spirits or souls – fully formed selves – who happen to live at the particular time and place which provides the conditions in which they do or don't then fulfil the potential that is naturally theirs. The first view, which can be summarized as a crude sociological determinism, was famously debunked by Sartre's comment to the effect that while Paul Valéry might indeed be a *petit-bourgeois*, not all *petit-bourgeois* were Valéry. The second view could be typified by the kind of hagiography which takes its subject as divinely aloof from the period that chanced to be that of his or her lifetime, and speculates, for instance, about what Shakespeare would have to say about video nasties, or what Coleridge would have to say about deconstruction, 'if they were with us now'.

Somewhere between these two poles, and utilizing elements of each to varying degrees, is the 'life and times' model whose two terms are posited as relatively independent of one another, but mutually influential. So, for instance, Virginia Woolf, it might be said, was the product of an upper-middle-class Victorian family combined with the Edwardian intellectual reaction against the nineteenth century; her genius (which is a given) must be seen in these contexts. Depending on whether the object of the work is primarily to celebrate its hero(ine) or to 'paint the portrait' of an age, or of a given milieu – whether, in other words, it is meant to mark out the subject as an exceptional or as a typical figure – the 'life' or the 'times' will be represented with more or less emphasis. (A variant worth noting, because it is characteristic of accounts of 'Bloomsbury', is the definition of an artistic or intellectual 'circle' around the several distinct 'personalities', or unique lives, which gave it its special flavour.)

We have seen how in Woolf's own case the many ways in which she is represented give rise to all the ambiguities of an 'exemplary' status, at once unique and representative. The primary difficulty with the 'life and times' model, and all the more with the exclusively 'life' (genius) or deterministic emphases of the initial polarity, is that it is static and cannot move outside what it takes as a given identity and unity in each of the two terms set next to each other. 'The nineteenth century' or 'the bourgeois family' are entities which, like billiard balls, are said to have knocked that other billiard ball,

Virginia Woolf, in particular directions; or, put the other way round, 'the twentieth century mind' or 'feminist thought' are said to have been deflected or straightened out by the impact of that same 'Virginia Woolf'. Or, to change the image: in the first example, she is like a *tabula rasa* receiving impressions, in the second she is the source or agent of what impresses itself upon other bodies of varying degrees of tangibility. Either Virginia Woolf is contaminated (or fertilized) from outside, or she is contaminating or fertilizing other entities: the identities of all the parties concerned are taken to be known in advance, but open to adverse or positive influence.

In the humanistic or romantic view of the subject, his 'originality' fulfils itself with the suppport of, or in spite of the constraints of, the 'time' – whether that is represented primarily in terms of material or intellectual ('spirit of the age') conditions. This is related to a form of argument which assesses historical individuals in terms of how far they did or did not manage to 'take a distance from', or 'escape from the restrictions of', their 'time'. The implied historical perspective is that of progressive enlightenment: we now know more than they did then, and can see those old beliefs for the superstitions that they were. Those who are deemed outstanding people are praised when they are seen to have broken away from their 'times', and excused, because they had no means of knowing any better, when they are seen to have fallen into the prejudices from which we have now, thankfully, moved on.

By making Orlando's life a matter of several hundred years, Woolf gives herself a perfect opportunity to tease out the underlying assumptions of biographical conventions concerning the identity of the subject through time and in relation to his or her milieux: 'Orlando had inclined herself naturally to the Elizabethan spirit, to the Restoration spirit, to the spirit of the eighteenth century, and had in consequence scarcely been aware of the change from one age to the other' (152). First, Orlando's progress or movement through the ages could be said to make of her/him a kind of Every(wo)man, the typical human enabling the narrative to explore the differences in the external containers of human subjectivity. This view is however undermined by what follows:

> But the spirit of the nineteenth century was antipathetic to her . . . For it is probable that the human spirit has its place in time assigned to it; some are born of this age, some of that; and now that Orlando was grown a woman, a year or two past thirty indeed, the lines of her character were fixed, and to bend them the wrong way was intolerable.
>
> (*O*, 152)

Here, humans are not average or typical, but unique or at least distinct types, whose essences are 'fixed' independently of the time of their life, if not of their time of life, which may or may not by propitious to their development or fulfilment. 'Fixed' summarizes the ambiguity of the negotiation between the two given entities of the spirit and the age: it can either be the self's arrival at the state of self-identity which will resolutely resist external pressures to change; or it can mean a lack of openness, a rigidity antipathetic to modification or influence from outside. The text leaves possible both interpretations: valorizing the autonomous self for which the outside is a source of violations, or valorizing the flexible and never fully settled self, for which the outside is the source of modifications and mouldings which do not mar a pre-given identity.

At some points, Orlando's biographer inclines to the first view, assuming a fixed 'core' of self: 'Orlando was in an extremely happy position; she need neither fight her age, nor submit to it; she was of it, yet remained herself' (167). At other points, there is no single self:

> So Orlando, at the turn by the barn, called 'Orlando?' with a note of interrogation in her voice and waited. Orlando did not come.
>
> 'All right then,' Orlando said, with the good humour people practise on these occasions; and tried another. For she had a great variety of selves to call upon, far more than we have been able to find room for, since a biography is considered complete if it merely accounts for six or seven selves, whereas a person may well have as many thousand.
>
> (*O*, 193)

This multiplication of selves is asociated first with Orlando's reaching (in the twentieth century) middle age, when 'Nothing is any longer one thing': a department store can suggest a different place and time (the earlier Turkish interlude) and there is a perpetual and vain attempt 'to synchronize the sixty or seventy different times which beat simultaneously in every normal human system' (191). This opens up a complex structure in which the self is not a unity – either through time or in opposition to the passage of time – but is constituted, and unevenly so, by layerings of times and sights impinging in disparate ways upon what is only 'the present moment' to the extent that it also engages with all those other 'moments'. It is only upon this 'disassembled' (192), multiple self that the semblance of unity is constructed: 'her mind regained the illusion of holding things within itself and she saw a cottage, a farmyard and four cows, all precisely lifesize' (192).

The passage in which this occurs, involving Orlando's shopping trip up to London and return by 'motor car' to her country seat, raises the further question of the relation of the multiple selves to historical periods. Is the disunity or disassembly of the self to be taken as specifically a phenomenon of middle age or of modernity? What is the relation between the comprehension of many historical periods in relation to the hypothetical 'present moment' and the comprehension, or attempted holding together, of the multiple 'selves' formed by the layered memories of the individual 'history'?

Everything is clear at a glance to the reader of the eighteenth-century city streets:

> She caught sight of a variety of painted signs swinging in the breeze and could form a rapid notion from what was painted on them of the tobacco, of the stuff, of the silk, of the gold, of the silver ware, of the gloves, of the perfumes, and of a thousand other articles which were sold within.
> (*O*, 104)

In the twentieth century, instead of this completeness and legibility, with the readily readable correspondence of the sign to its recognizable, conventional meaning, the signs speed by – or are sped by – too fast to be comprehended, taken in:

> Applejohn and Applebed, Undert–. Nothing could be seen whole or read from start to finish. What was seen

> begun – like two friends starting to meet each other across the street – was never seen ended. After twenty minutes the body and mind were like scraps of torn paper tumbling from a sack and, indeed, the process of motoring fast out of London so much resembles the chopping up small of identity which precedes unconsciousness and perhaps death itself that it is an open question in what sense Orlando can be said to have existed at the present moment.
>
> (*O*, 192)

The impossibility of concluding or completing – 'was never seen ended' – is a direct result, in this model, of the sights to which the body and mind react in the attempt to make a whole meaning of them. With the breaking off of the 'Undert–', it is as if even 'death itself' cannot be allowed to have a decent end. (Woolf here once again renders less finely satisfying the street meeting of the couple getting into the taxi in *A Room of One's Own*: the 'friends' in this passage never come together at all.) The world is presented as something to be read, as a giant sign consisting of an unending series of minute portions. The second passage posits a mirror relationship between the readability of the things of the world and that of identity: 'body and mind' themselves become like messageless fragments, 'scraps of torn paper'.

The continuation of the episode, part of which was quoted above, gives some restoration or acquisition of the unity heralded as lacking:

> Indeed we should have given her over for a person entirely disassembled were it not that here, at last, one green screen was held out on the right, against which the little bits of paper fell more slowly; and then another was held out on the left so that one could see the separate scraps now turning over by themselves in the air; and then green screens were held continuously on either side, so that her mind regained the illusion of holding things within itself and she saw a cottage, a farmyard and four cows, all precisely lifesize.
>
> (*O*, 192)

The 'scraps' slow down in favour of pastoral verdancy – the 'green screen' a cinema version, perhaps, of Marvell's seventeenth-century 'green thought in a green shade'.[4] This reinforces the implied return from the modern city to an earlier age and a simpler, more wholesome life represented by the farmyard. But the language remains as open-ended as the literally impossible but nevertheless harmonizing 'green thought' itself. The 'green screens' are still the stuff of a spectacle or painting – Orlando's personal cinema viewed from the car, providing her mind with the 'illusion' of holding things within itself.

Oldness, unity, pastoral simplicity, far from being the pre-fragmentary original to the 'disassembled' modern city and modern self, only function as what is connoted by the 'green screens', which are just as much signs or pictures as those advertising themselves as such on the city streets. This fragile unification of Orlando's dispersed selves is no less effective for being derived from a spectacle which is of exactly the same order as the fragmenting vision from which it is differentiated. The question then closes with the problem of 'in what sense Orlando can be said to have existed at the present moment', for historical periods get represented as moving from unity and wholeness to fragmentation and multiplicity (or the other way round) in just the same way as does the 'self' in its passage to the complexities (or fixities) of middle age. 'The present moment' in a life or in history, or according to historical differences in what structures the human self, is only the name of the point from which there appears to have been a past: it is thus necessarily a 'moment' of division, not of presence in the sense of immediacy or self-sufficiency: a moment of separation rather than separateness.

This analysis could however be turned against itself and placed as being a characteristically modern account of both history and subjectivity, founded (or unfounded) on fragmentation rather than unity, and declaring the latter to be nothing more than an illusion usually underpinned by some reference to a prior (or future) time of plenitude. The other story of the fragmentary modern subject would hold that there has indeed been change in both the forms of subjectivity and the cohesiveness or readability of the world through different historical periods. Orlando's multiple selves and fragmented experience would fit, in this description, with a 'spirit of the age' expressed in precisely this disunity or (on the 'object' side) with a world differing from its antecedents as does a car journey from a train journey, or a department store from an umbrella shop. Trains follow fixed routes with known destinations; cars take infinitely modifiable routes according to the whim of individual drivers. Department stores sell any number of heterogeneous goods without an umbrella category to unite them: the casual modern shopper will wander round without a definite object, where the customer used to go to a specific shop for a specific category of goods to make an already determined purchase.

Getting into a lift in the London department store Marshall and Snelgrove's, Orlando reflects: 'The very fabric of life now . . . is magic. In the eighteenth century, we knew how everything was done; but here I rise through the air; I listen to voices in America; I see men flying – but how it's done, I can't even begin to wonder. So my belief in magic returns' (187–8). The rising elevator, entered 'for the good reason that the door stood open', is rapidly connected as a new invention to the telephone and the aeroplane, which are said not only to be responsible for new modes of thinking, but to be experienced in the form of 'magic' – the very opposite of the technological rationality which gives rise to their performance – and conceived as a 'return' to a pre-industrial form of thinking.

At the same time these new, magical objects have become the everyday framework for the way in which the world is perceived. Back in the country mansion:

> The old grey walls of the house looked like a scraped new photograph; she heard the loud speaker condensing on the terrace a dance tune that people were listening to in the red velvet opera house at Vienna. Braced and strung up by the present moment she was also strangely afraid, as if whenever the gulf of time gaped and let a second through some unknown danger might come with it.
>
> (*O*, 200)

The once feudal establishment has now dwindled to being the image of an image (it is 'like' a photograph) and the indifferent site of the reproduction of music performed at a different time and in a different place. Like Pointz Hall in *Between the Acts*, it represents a transformation of the ancestral territory to a stage set: from being a centre radiating outwards, it has lost its separate identity and can offer Orlando no such fixity of view or unity of experience. The photograph and the gramophone indicate, in this analysis, the separation of what might once have been unified sensory perceptions, in touch with nature and tradition.

But *Orlando* does not allow that this historical model of subjective, experiential change should be taken as more correct, any more than the novel endorses the generalization of the model of the multiple self. Nor does it imply a decline (or a rise) in the stature of human life. The hypothetical unity at the beginning is shown to be just as much a matter of (literally) received ideas as the modern, fragmentary forms, involving the taking in of multiplied impressions by a subject who has no unity or centre. This is clear as we have seen from the repeated foregrounding on the one hand of the function of languages and literary styles in shaping the understanding and perception of reality (in the nineteenth century, 'sentences swelled, adjectives multiplied' (143)), and on the other of the codes of biographical and historical writing. Each of these is exemplified in the references to the typical stories through which 'life' is understood at different times. It is here that the effect of Orlando's two sexes is revealed as the last 'illusion', and the first, which the narrator succeeds in showing up.

9 Partings

> People of my generation know now exactly what war is – its positive horrors of death and destruction, wounds and pain and bereavement and brutality, but also its negative emptiness and desolation of personal and cosmic boredom, the feeling that one is endlessly waiting in a dirty, grey railway station waiting-room, with nothing to do but wait endlessly for the next catastrophe.[1]

> The story ends without any point to it. But I have not told you this anecdote to illustrate either my own ingenuity or the pleasure of travelling from Richmond to Waterloo.
>
> *CE*, I: 324

Between the Acts could be seen as the culmination of Woolf's recurrent and persistent explorations of conceptions of history-writing. To call it the culmination is immediately of course to beg all the questions the novel raises. Culmination implies a purposeful climb towards a peak, an end that concludes rather than merely being the last of a series, as with the alphabet. It implies a shape, a structure in relation to which the end makes sense: the whole can be interpreted and comprehended. The culmination can be seen as a logical, though not perhaps the sole, rational outcome of the beginning. Ironically, too, there is a contradiction built into the claim that Woolf's last novel (it was written in 1940, just before her death) is the final, most relentless achievement of that questioning and undermining of literary and historical narrative forms which she had been practising throughout. For that is immediately to reconstruct Woolf's writing as a history with a logical development, coherently narrated, when the end point of that development is said to be a recognition of the impossibility of any such story.

The title on its own casts doubts on such constructions. 'Between' is not terminal but connective (or disjunctive); the 'acts' of a play indicate problems of form and fictionality which undermine the certainties of historical actions and knowledge. The novel puts the question of history in several ways. First, by the structure: with Miss La Trobe's pageant the focus, it is that of a play within a novel, and plays within that play. Each period of English history is successively represented by satirical vignettes done in the style of well-known literary genres of the time. For the audience, the recognition of particular historical ages is itself mediated through literary history as cliché, and for the reader of the novel this is taken one stage further, since the village setting itself alludes to the well-established genre of English pastoral.

Second, and obviously, by the setting of the action, or of the 'between', 'on a June day in 1939' (*BA*, 75), inviting the reader to supply for the acts the two world wars and to understand what separates them as no more than an interlude. Fighting would then be the chief human act (or performance), and anything else just an interval or pause between its occurrences. But the summer of 1939 epitomized in the fictional representation of a fictional representation of history, leaves open all the uncertainty as to its potential for generalization: whether the date can be taken as emblematic or symptomatic of an invariable condition of historical suspense 'between' latent or potential acts of aggression.

This becomes all the more unsettling when '1939' is compared to '1910'. For one of the connotations attached to the change hypothetically marked 'in or about December, 1910' (*CE*, I: 324) is the difference in 'human character' that appears after the 1914–18 war. By 1939, this war can appear to have been not 'the war to end all wars', but the First World War of a potentially endless series, or else nothing more, or nothing less, than a dress rehearsal for what really will be the final catastrophe.[2] In this regard, the period since can seem to have been only the interval 'between', before the next or the last decisive event.

Third, the novel questions the conceptualization of personal and social histories by focusing on the continuities and disjunctions in what goes to make up, or to appear to make up, an individual and a social group, and the sense of a personal or collective past. As in *The Years* or *Orlando*, in different ways, the representation of a personal past – and by extension, of a possible future – comes to be related to the terms in which historical or cultural change can be conceived.

Beyond its foregrounding of history as representational, the novel works with conflicting conceptions of historical time. Within the play, the acts mark out a series of distinct periods, each with its own style of language and typical scenes, one following another in a sequence of discrete and disconnected forms up until 'The Present Time. Ourselves' (178). Because the acts are separate, the logic of their linking is unspecified:

> It was an awkward moment. How to make an end?
>
> (*BA*, 194)

> How difficult to come to any conclusion! She wished they would hurry on with the next scene. She liked to leave a theatre knowing exactly what was meant.
>
> (*BA*, 164)

In personal life, the same demand for rational connections, for a meaning to explain the logic of the series, comes through. Giles Oliver might have been a farmer:

> But he was not given his choice. So one thing led to another; and the conglomeration of things pressed you flat.
>
> (*BA*, 47)

Besides serial history, there is history as recurrence or repetition: not one different thing after another, but the same and the same returning. This is figured first in the situation of the annual event of the village play:

> 'I've been nailing the placard on the Barn,' she said, giving him a little pat on the shoulder.
>
> The words were like the first peal of a chime of bells. At the first peal, you hear the second; as the second peals, you hear the third. So when Isa heard Mrs. Swithin say: 'I've been nailing the placard on the Barn,' she knew she would say next:
>
> 'For the pageant.'
>
> (*BA*, 21–2)

The formulaic and predetermined repetition of words marks a different temporality from a third type between these two, involving continuities and infinitesimal changes within a basically stable order. Family reproduction is the paradigm here: 'Many old men had only their India. She in her striped dress continued him' (18). The Barn, the old house, the names of the 'indigenous' villagers, signify a permanent, virtually unchanging form – in which different figures are inscribed from generation to generation, from time to time. This household time is not only designated by the father's name: 'fifteen years ago, before Sands came, in the time of Jessie Pook' (33) brings family history downstairs to a succession of cooks' reigns, replacing the father's name with a different kind of nominal shift like what is designated, on the previous page, as a 'kitchen change'.[3]

At the extreme of temporal variants, there is the complete absence of time, whether repetitive or progressive:

> All's equal there. Unblowing, ungrowing are the roses there. Change is not; nor the mutable and lovable; nor greetings nor partings.
>
> (*BA*, 155)

This is timelessness, a state outside history and natural cycles, the limit case against which the other forms of temporality are measured. But the same challenge to the distinction between serial time and repetitive time is produced be the sound of a machine: 'Only the tick, tick, tick of the gramophone held them together' (154). This 'tick, tick, tick' points to the arbitrary separation and joining of the regular temporal units against which the significant 'moments' in a life or in history appear to stand out. The ticks can be heard as either repetition or sequence, and thus confound the difference between repetition and linearity.

The undoing of any stable conception of time on which to peg a conception of history or historical change is thus carried out more radically even than in *Orlando* or *To the Lighthouse*; it is figured as much by the comments of members of the play's audience as in the double structure of play and novel. Old Mrs Swithin responds to the vignette of Victorian domesticity towards the end of the play:

> 'I don't believe there ever were such people. Only you and me dressed differently.'
>
> 'You don't believe in history,' said William.
>
> (*BA*, 174–5)

The Victorian age generally features in Woolf's writing for that which the new generation had to repudiate, or shake off, in order to assert a difference. But here, as with the episodic costume changes of *Orlando*, the nineteenth century offers no more significant difference than that of an alternative type of dress convention.

The possibility of an 'overall' identity, despite appearances to the contrary, between people and between historical periods, is repeatedly evoked in *Between the Acts* through this image of the clothes change, and notably with reference to the quick alterations effected by the characters in the play:

> 'Perhaps she'll reach the present, if she skips. . . . D'you think people change? Their clothes, of course. . . . But I meant ourselves . . . Clearing out a cupboard, I found my father's old top hat. . . . But ourselves – do we change?'
>
> (*BA*, 120–1; ellipses Woolf's)

> Then he saw her face change, as if she had got out of one dress and put on another.
>
> (*BA*, 105)

The change of clothes is so obvious ('of course') that it may slip by unnoticed: here the dress change is logically prior to that of the face. In a reversal of the conventional order, it is clothes, by implication, which make the woman whose smile may then follow this mutation: instead of clothes implying an inner change, the changed face indicates the (metaphorically deeper, underlying) truth that the clothes have changed. Recalling the ambiguities of *Orlando*, the remark raises the possibility that people's changing is more a matter of clothes than selves. This could mean that it is only apparent, on the surface: that what passes for a fundamental 'shift' in subjective identity is only dress-deep. It could also mean that the terms are reversed: that identity is indeed manufactured by what is normally taken to be only the superficial expression of an inner truth.

This ambivalence as to the relation between the two terms potentially turns inside out the priority of part to whole in the figure which makes the clothing an aspect of the person. It is repeated in the novel's frequent play on the meaning of the word *part*. The 'part' in *Between the Acts* is first of all the stage part; it is also the part as opposed to the whole; and it is attached, by various forms, to the words having to do with 'part' as a verb: to leave, to separate.

The villagers act parts in the play that represents their own history; in the transformation where they become, for a day, Queen Elizabeth and the lords and ladies that the village shopkeeper and publican are not, the usual hierarchies are in appearance reversed. But this only exposes their resilience. Between the acts, in the interval where common folk and gentry take tea together in the Barn, the orders of precedence remain: 'It's all my eye about democracy,' says Mrs Manresa (102). At the same time, the scripting of the play indicates a lack of autonomy for individual actors, all subject to the whims of the author, Miss La Trobe. This is true also of the audience, before which the successive stages of English history pass as a spectacle in which they have no part.

In this version of things, the fictionality of history and of the self appears as negative, as a travesty of the notion of individual or national agency as opposed to a puppet-like powerlessness which is revealed as such. But on the other side, there is the foregrounding of the stage figures as the image of something more than what Mrs Swithin calls 'this daily round; this going up and down stairs' (152):

> What a small part I've had to play! But you've made me feel I could have played . . . Cleopatra.
>
> (*BA*, 153; ellipsis in text)

Where all the world's a stage, the taking of a different role might represent not a further degradation of a dwindled self, since there is no self prior to the acting or the costume, but a heightening or access of power. This is how Miss La Trobe understands the old lady's admiration:

> 'I might have been – Cleopatra,' Miss La Trobe repeated. 'You've stirred in me my unacted part,' she meant. . . .
>
> 'You've twitched the invisible strings,' was what the old lady meant; and revealed – of all people – Cleopatra! Glory possessed her. Ah, but she was not merely a twitcher of individual strings; she was one who seethes wandering bodies and floating voices in a cauldron, and makes rise up from its amorphous mass a re-created world. Her moment was on her – her glory.
>
> (*BA*, 153)

In taking herself to have bestowed on Mrs Swithin her 'unacted part', Miss La Trobe acquires her own: Cleopatra's glory makes heroines of them both, makes them the same in the moment which endows them with a fictional stature of uniqueness.

The 're-created world' suggests a different sense of parts: as fragments of a possible whole. These parts can also be read in a double way. In the last section of the play, 'Present Time', when the boundaries between spectators and spectacle are abolished through the parade of mirrors by actors moving among the audience, the voice of anonymity declaims:

> *Look at ourselves, ladies and gentlemen! then at the wall; and ask how's this wall, the great wall, which we call, perhaps miscall, civilization, to be built by* (here the mirrors flicked and flashed) *orts, scraps and fragments like ourselves?*
>
> (*BA*, 188)

What breaks down here is not only the comfortable separation of spectator from spectacle, but also the supposed collectivity of 'civilization', of 'ourselves'. 'Look at ourselves', instead of the grammatically more complete 'Let's look at ourselves', allows for the possibility that it is uttered by a subject which is not included in 'ourselves'. It thus repeats the division implied by the 'orts, scraps and fragments' of which 'we' are constituted – or which 'ourselves' are 'like'. 'Ourselves' figure waveringly and fragmentarily in the mirrors, as much external to the observer as is the voice of admonishment or the 'wall' established to represent 'civilization'. Syntax and diction reinforce this effect: the 'voice' is abruptly broken in two by the parenthesis, and the 'orts, scraps and fragments' work almost formulaically. All three words are semantically interchangeable; the 'orts' are archaic and add to the incantatory suggestion.

This 'wall' is itself an ambiguous figure, pointing back, first of all, to the wall of *A Midsummer Night's Dream*, and thus to another (parodic) play within a play, as here it is part of a play within a play within a novel. Formal allusiveness is joined, or soldered, to the literal repetition of the (illusion of an) objective wall on the stage. The difference between the comically exaggerated function in the earlier play – to mark the separation of Pyramus and Thisbe – and its place here – to stand for something called civilization – draws attention, from a different angle, to the vulnerability of 'Civilization (the wall) in ruins' (181): the wall is less a solid substantial identity, than something which serves as a partition; it is less a thing than a 'between'. So now, contrary to first appearances, the wall of civilization joins or rejoins the condition of the 'orts, scraps and fragments' of 'ourselves' from which it seemed to stand apart. It fails, after all, to supply a wholeness making up for their disunity, covering that over by standing as the unifying symbol of 'ourselves', a collectivity.

The 'parts' of the fragments without any whole are not far away – in an adjacent passage – from the 'parting' of separation:

> 'The play's over, I take it,' muttered Colonel Mayhew, retrieving his hat. 'It's time . . .'
>
> But before they had come to any common conclusion, a voice asserted itself. Whose voice it was no one knew. It

came from the bushes – a megaphonic, anonymous, loud-speaking affirmation. The voice said:

Before we part, ladies and gentlemen, before we go . . .

(*BA*, 186–7; ellipses in text)

'Coming' to a conclusion would be a prerequisite for 'parting', it is implied. The 'common' end precedes or determines, in the normal course of things to which the passage alludes, the parting of ourselves. *Between the Acts* never offers a common or uncommon, shared or singular conclusion: the interval does not end. Unlike the rhythmic, wave-like pattern of a potentially harmonious order offered in others of Woolf's novels, here – though there are such passages from time to time – 'parting' – leaving and separating – has already taken precedence over the possibility of a joint arrival or shared meaning.

This 'suspended' state is repeatedly evoked in the language of *Between the Acts*, and especially in the middle section, during the play's first interval, when Giles goes off on his own and comes across a horrific animal pairing:

> There, couched in the grass, curled in an olive green ring, was a snake. Dead? No, choked with a toad in its mouth. The snake was unable to swallow; the toad was unable to die. A spasm made the ribs contract; blood oozed. It was birth the wrong way round – a monstrous inversion.
>
> (*BA*, 99)

At first sight, this configuration might look like a primitive, perverse type of miscegenation, a union across the boundaries of the species. It is one of a number of images in the novel where love and hate, aggressivity and desire, seem indistinguishable, or coexist, or rapidly succeed one another.

In particular, there is the final scene with Giles and Isa, after the others have gone to bed:

> Alone, enmity was bared; also love. Before they had slept, they must fight; after they had fought, they would embrace.
>
> (*BA*, 219)

Here there is an oscillation from one extreme to the other (enmity/love; fighting/embracing; separation/fusion) which, in its very repetition, effectively reduces the distinction between the two states to one of position in relation to a pendulum's swing:

> There were only two emotions: love; and hate. There was no need to puzzle out the plot. Perhaps that was what Miss La Trobe meant when she cut this knot in the centre?
>
> Don't bother about the plot: the plot's nothing.
>
> (*BA*, 90–1)

In the alternation between loving and hating, cyclically repeated, the content of the two seems to have ceased to matter, since their difference is a matter of position rather than substance. The 'between' is all; and so the shock of the snake and the toad is in part its exposure of what the novel represents as the common condition. The animals are stuck in the middle of a process which should culminate (indifferently) in fusion or death; the impasse is horrible because it is an impasse, and this then produces the appearance of 'inversion' and monstrosity, an impossible 'between' that cannot be viewed with the equanimity that would make it a recognizable stage of a movement from one pole to the other.

> They sat exposed. The machine ticked. There was no music. The horns of cars on the high road were heard. And the swish of trees. They were neither one thing nor the other; neither Victorians nor themselves. They were suspended, without being, in limbo. Tick, tick, tick went the machine.
>
> (*BA*, 178)

> The ticking stopped. A dance tune was put on the machine. In time to it, Isa hummed: 'What do I ask? To fly away, from night and day, and issue where – no partings are – but eye meets eye – and . . .'
>
> (*BA*, 83)

'No partings': at once no differences, no splittings or separations of wholes; and at the same time no leaving, no goings away, no departure of one thing from another. But 'night and day', as the vestiges of temporal alternation, have also ceased to mark the regularity of their difference. Where 'eye meets eye', or 'I' meets 'I', the difference between 'you' and 'I' dissolves into indistinguishability. This is what Isa wants from romantic love; it is also what she wants when the object of her desire is not in sight: 'She looked round. She could not see the man in grey, the gentleman farmer; nor anyone known to her. "That the waters should cover me," she added, "of the wishing well"' (103). An earlier scene foreshadows and anticipates the play's exposure, with the cracked mirrors, of the fragility of 'what I call myself' (149) as of what 'we call, perhaps miscall, civilization' (188). Isa sits in front of her mirror in the morning.

> Inside the glass, in her eyes, she saw what she had felt overnight for the ravaged, the silent, the romantic gentleman farmer. 'In love', was in her eyes. But outside, on the washstand, on the dressing-table, among the silver boxes and tooth-brushes, was the other love; love for her husband, the stockbroker – 'The father of my children,' she added, slipping into the cliché conveniently provided by fiction. Inner love was in her eyes; outer love on the dressing-table.
>
> (*BA*, 14)

Isa's own love is split between the romantic love of the farmer, linked to her own image in the mirror, and the outer love of property and paternity which enables the persistence of conventions and 'civilization'. The 'cliché' is both formulaic and, radically, a 'fiction' – for, as Odysseus's son was the first in western literature to point out, paternity, unlike maternity, can never be positively demonstrated.[4]

The two loves, one of harmonious indifference, 'where eye meets eye', and one of the social order, the conventional respect for the father and his property, are asymmetrical. The first, despite its unifying tendency, goes nowhere, is changeless; the second is that of historical time, of the masculine 'fiction' of a stable line handed down, and on, and with interest, from one generation to the next. It might appear that the mirror image of the woman in love supplies a natural completeness and one-to-one fusion that the separated, artificial paternal love does not. But the inverted commas of being 'in love' already mark the state as being as much of a cliché as the props that support that 'other love'. 'In love' is what Isa reads in the reflection in the mirror, as if falling in love with the image of herself as in love. She is parted not just by the difference between the two loves but by the one which seems to offer an image of unification. This double discrepancy – within the image of unification and in its difference from the paternal line – could be likened to the division between the railway passenger and the distant image of the wife and child in *To the Lighthouse*. From the situation of the woman, the disjunctions appear in even sharper relief.[5]

Later, this nexus of erotic investments is repeated, but with a difference, when Isa's husband Giles returns from London and joins the picnic party before the play:

> 'He is my husband,' Isabella thought, as they nodded across the bunch of many-coloured flowers. 'The father of my children.' It worked, that old cliché; she felt pride; and affection; then pride again in herself, whom he had chosen. It was a shock to find, after the morning's look in the glass, and the arrow of desire shot through her last night by the gentleman farmer, how much she felt when he came in, not a dapper city gent, but a cricketer, of love; and of hate.
>
> (*BA*, 47–8)

The father is returned to the place previously occupied by the lover. Her 'pride . . . in herself, whom he had chosen' now mirrors the looks at herself 'in love'. What she loves, as loving her, is still the man of the country, not the city – the 'gentleman farmer' or cricketer, not the 'dapper city gent'. But this is also how Giles, the husband, sees himself ideally: 'Given the choice, he would have chosen to farm' (47). The 'arrow of desire', another 'cliché conveniently provided by fiction' (14), is shot by a man who represents to Isa what her husband failed to become. Her image of him corresponds to his own, but the incompatibility between the two holds fast, through the unbridgeable semicolon 'of love; and of hate'.

Yet from Giles's point of view, his appearance in country gear at this juncture represents not so much his 'unacted' part (153) as a concession, at the sight of the prestigious Manresa automobile, to 'the ghost of convention': 'So the car touched his training. He must change. And he came into the dining room looking like a cricketer, in flannels' (46). His 'change' from one part to another is closer to the cliché of the conventional script than to the transformation into a more authentic identity. Giles switches from one role (the city gent) to another.

There is thus no truer self against which to measure the succession of roles and costumes (historical change reduced to the costume changes of 'Only you and me dressed differently' (172)), and the structure of misrecognitions of 'what I call myself' or of 'what we call, perhaps miscall, civilization'. In *Between the Acts* both this English civilization and its subjects turn out to be constituted by a grand illusion none the less binding ('It worked, the old cliché') for that: 'So one thing led to another; and the conglomeration of things pressed you flat; held you fast, like a fish in water' (47). But, as in *Orlando*, it is not clear whether or not this way of perceiving history and identity is itself modern, and thereby retrospectively reconstructs the way in which every other historical period is imagined.

The toad and serpent locked in a combat with no issue can thus be taken as connected to the limbo of 'a summer's day in June, 1939'. Here, or now, it is not a matter of marking a date when 'human character changed', for 'human character' on this reading never existed in the first place or the first time. Rather, historical narrative has come to a halt altogether and the progressive story it might once have told is exposed in the verbal residues of what is offered as nothing more than the formulaic conventions and functioning cliché of acted roles, and of history rehashed as a disconnected mixture of literary parodies and allusions. '1939' might be situated in some sense on the border between a world of secure histories and a world of allusion, cliché and fragments.[6]

The 'between' of '1939' marks, if it marks at all, an end to the possibility of endings. There is no plot and no conclusion, no triumph of love or of hate, no resolution; and the terms of these oppositions themselves fall apart in the break-up of the syntax:

> The gramophone gurgled *Unity – Dispersity*. It gurgled *Un . . . dis* . . . And ceased.
>
> (*BA*, 201)

But the end of the novel – 'Then the curtain rose. They spoke.' (219) – also points to something to come after, something next. 'Birth the wrong way round' (99) may then acquire a new kind of suggestion: more than a grotesque perversion of the order of things, it is what interrupts that order, rendering it unrecognizable and strange. This peculiar *partage* is close to an announcement made by Derrida beginning *Of Grammatology*: 'The future can only be anticipated in the form of an absolute danger. It is what breaks absolutely with normality as constituted and can only be proclaimed, *presented*, as a sort of monstrosity'.[7] What departs from the present scheme is inconceivable within it, and so can only look now like a monster. Miss La Trobe's production has none of the belated unifying quality of Lily Briscoe's painting, but leaves entirely open-ended the relations of past, present and future, and the continuation of the paternal lines of tradition. It could be that what has gone in *Between the Acts*, or after '1939', is the possibility of a cultural history with a fixed destination, and that the way is then open for a different, but necessarily unimaginable, kind of story.

10 The Dotted Line

> But . . . I had said but too often. One cannot go on saying but.
>
> *ROO*, 95; ellipsis in text

> And it is to end with three dots . . . so.
>
> *D*, 3: 131

> For what can be simpler than to join the society to which this guinea has just been contributed? On the face of it, how easy, how simple; but in the depths, how difficult, how complicated. . . . What possible doubts, what possible hesitations can those dots stand for? What reason or what emotion can make us hesitate to become members of a society whose aims we approve, to whose funds we have contributed? It may be neither reason nor emotion, but something more profound and fundamental than either. It may be difference. Different we are, as facts have proved, both in sex and in education.
>
> (*TG*, 103)

Like *Between the Acts*, *Three Guineas* is full of 'those dots' and the question of what they might 'stand for'. One of the first things the three dots suggest is the difficulty of concluding; there follow, then, a few points (or dots) to continue this exploration of the various 'lines' in Woolf's work.

A Signing on the Dotted Line

Three Guineas complicates what might appear at first sight, or 'on the face of it' (103), to be the simple matter of a woman offering her financial support to a man's request for help in preventing war. Subscribing to the common cause – by signing her name and by contributing her guinea – is shown to be anything but a straightforward business. On the one hand, women have been excluded by men from the education and money which give access to freedom; on the other hand, it is this same 'patriarchal' society which has produced the aggression and war for the elimination of which women are now being asked to add their efforts. The difference of the sexes ('different we are' (103)) is said to be a result of male tyranny; at the same time, it gives women the position of 'outsiders' with a different view of the world from that of men: 'though we look at the same things, we see them differently' (5). And so to commit herself without qualifications – without masculine credentials and without making any conditions – would run the risk of assimilation, of the loss of a different perspective. The quotation above goes on:

> And it is from that difference, as we have already said, that our help can come, if help we can, to protect liberty, to prevent war. But if we sign this form which implies a promise to become active members of your society, it would seem that we must lose that difference and therefore sacrifice that help.
>
> (*TG*, 103–4)

B Omissions

> Determined to do my duty by her as reader if she would do her duty by me as writer, I turned the page and read . . . I am sorry to break off so abruptly. Are there no men present?
>
> (*ROO*, 78; ellipsis in text)

Conventionally, three dots indicate something left out, of indeterminate length. Woolf's ellipses point towards what is omitted because it cannot be said: because it is not permitted, and/or because it is not assimilable to the surrounding prose. Here, an 'awkward break' (*ROO*, 66) is deliberately marked, and implies something in Mary Carmichael's writing omitted and silenced by her woman reader as being in some way 'unsuited' (*ROO*, 73) for a man to hear.

In the third essay of *The Pargiters*, the link is made with the unspeakable nature of sexual violence:

> There is, as the three dots used after the sentence, 'He unbuttoned his clothes . . .' testify, a convention, supported by law, which forbids, whether rightly or wrongly, any plain description of the sight that Rose, in common with many other little girls, saw under the lamp post by the pillar box in the dusk of that March evening.
>
> (*P*, 51)[1]

The only strategy for saying it is to say that it is that which cannot be said: to draw attention to the three dots. In *Three Guineas*, Woolf describes the unspoken questions and '"strong emotion"' aroused in a 'bi-sexual private conversation' (128) by the mention of women's admission to the professions:

> Intellectually, there is a strong desire either to be silent; or to change the conversation; to drag in, for example, some old family servant, called Crosby, perhaps, whose dog Rover has died . . . and so evade the issue and lower the temperature.
>
> But what analysis can we attempt of the emotions on the other side of the table – your side? Often, to be candid, while we are talking about Crosby, we are asking questions – hence a certain flatness in the dialogue – about you.
>
> (*TG*, 129; ellipsis Woolf's)

The questions that are not uttered but parenthetically suggested – between the dashes – are those for which the dialogue between men and women has no place, and no time: they cannot be represented in its terms. Hence even the conversation of the 'private' house is regulated by the more public 'society' which Woolf identifies as patriarchal. Since the woman is by definition left out of this patriarchy, there is no room for her in its language, which is why she must take up a position as outsider, in a room of her own. The three dots signpost this other place and these other questions which are excluded with such force ('strong emotions') and which are unassimilable to the public/private dialogue between the sexes.

C Fits and Stops

What the three dots stand for does not fit in with the sentence. Woolf regularly alludes to women's lack of adaptation to their allotted social and linguistic place:

> Inevitably we look upon society, so kind to you, so harsh to us, as an ill-fitting form that distorts the truth; deforms the mind; fetters the will.
>
> (*TG*, 105)

> It was a sentence that was unsuited for a woman's use.
>
> (*ROO*, 73)

What fits or is suitable suggests both convenience and propriety. There is a resistance to women's writing which is built into the very structure of syntax ('That is a man's sentence' (*ROO*, 73)) and into the structure of a society which will not take women as equals. What women write will be unfitting. The male sentence is not for women, and yet she is condemned to using it, however ineptly.[2]

The three dots also raise doubts about the sentence's completeness: there is no 'full' stop, no point at which it ends, to form a self-contained whole. The sentence does not conclude, but leaves loose ends, hints at something more which is not all sewn together: something without fit or finish.

D Breaks and Continuities

The alternation in the dotted line of spots and white spaces is a graphic representation of the minimal sequence of time. As with the gramophone's 'tick, tick, tick' in *Between the Acts*, it leaves suspended the question of whether this alternation is repetition or progression, waves or procession – or whether such oppositions are themselves inadequate. One dot after another, the dots appear against the background of the white paper that separates them as different, and by the same token shows them up as identical. One dot after another is the procession, or repetition, of the waves, or night and day, or the years; of historical or biographical periods. And 'periods' carry the same ambiguity, being at once full stops (dots, points that mark a break) and sentences (phases, extended units).

The dotted line is a line that is not joined up, that shows up its gaps. It challenges the firmness of the solid black line, or points out the arbitrariness of a masculine line of progress, as in Mr Ramsay's halted steps along the alphabet of intellectual attainment. At the same time, the absence of any line, of any assimilation to the prescribed directions of social and linguistic identity, would imply a chaos of pure dottiness. Woolf's dots are fitted inside the sentences they disturb and deprive of self-evidence, and so succeed in disturbing them. In her novels, the 'fit' of madness – Septimus Smith in *Mrs Dalloway*, Rachel Vinrace in *The Voyage Out* – inverts and jeopardizes the security of the 'fit' of conformity, of fitting in. Off the rails, the sufferer's different place makes the line of normality and convention appear as such. It is in this context – against the dominant masculine lines of English history and the English novel – that the 'orts, scraps and fragments' (*BA*, 188) of Woolf's texts acquire their own force.[3]

E Between the Lines

The dotted line inserted within the main line is therefore open, drawing attention to what it cannot accommodate, what it must leave out. In *Three Guineas*, Woolf refers to the partial 'hints and fragments' (77) which are the only source of evidence.

> But let us go on looking – if not at the lines, then between the lines of biography. And we find, between the lines of their husbands' biographies, so many women practising

> – but what are we to call the profession that consists in bringing nine or ten children into the world, the profession which consists in running a house, nursing an invalid, visiting the poor and the sick, tending here an old father, there an old mother? – there is no name and there is no pay for that profession.
>
> (*TG*, 77)

The sentence describing the hidden meaning 'between' the manifest lines of men's biographies itself breaks off for lack of a name to speak the 'profession' of the woman to be found there.

Exploring the interstices and interrupting the seeming continuities of discourse are among Woolf's favourite strategies: those of the woman in the corner who raises a doubt as to patriarchal centralities. 'Interruption' – 'breaking in between' – is practised and advocated repeatedly as a form of feminist questioning, as in the extended 'but' of *A Room of One's Own*. *Three Guineas*, after all, is nothing else than a rigorous dismantling of the overlooked implications of an apparently innocuous request for funds to work for peace. Interruption is also a syntactic device, characterized by Woolf's parenthetical style:

> Moreover, in a hundred years, I thought, reaching my own doorstep, women will have ceased to be the protected sex. Logically they will take part in all the activities and exertions that were once denied them. The nursemaid will heave coal. The shopwoman will drive an engine. All assumptions founded on the facts observed when women were the protected sex will have disappeared – as, for example (here a squad of soldiers marched down the street), that women and clergy and gardeners live longer than other people.
>
> (*ROO*, 40)

If there were any doubt as to the send-up of images of a socialist utopia implied in the first part, the parenthetical squad of soldiers quickly dissipates it, restoring the status quo, or rather demonstrating that the problem of male 'protection' of women is not so rapidly dealt with. What ought to be an inessential detail, adding to the realistic effect of the narrator's pause at her front door in mid-meditation, completely destroys the security of the visions within which it is placed.

Interlude

The Waves is Woolf's most relentless study of the impasses between all the possible interpretations of the relations between the 'dots': of how, or whether, distinct 'moments' or times can be linked into a line. And the alternation in this text of italicized 'interludes' (the term is Woolf's (*D*, 4: 34)) and extended dramatic monologues attributed successively to the six personae leaves unstated, and thus open to any interpretation, the form of the connection between them. The phases of the year and of the sun's passage through the sky, which the interludes describe, can be taken as analogical to the successive stages in the lives of the six characters, but this is never explicitly stated. What is suggested, rather, in the characters' various pronouncements, is an insistent push towards the making of one connection or another, of deciding upon the relationship, or lack of it, 'between' characters, moments, words, sentences and (by implication) parts of the text. Without some such connection, identity collapses, as it does for Rhoda; and yet only for the mind that does not see the normal sequence as natural can any kind of question emerge:

> 'Chaos, detail return. I am no longer amazed by names written over shop-windows. I do not feel Why hurry? Why catch trains? The sequence returns; one thing leads to another – the usual order.
>
> 'Yes, but I still resent the usual order. I will not let myself be made yet to accept the sequence of things. . . .' (*W*, 104)

> 'I cannot make one moment merge in the next. To me they are all violent, all separate; and if I fall under the shock of the leap of the moment you will be on me, tearing me to pieces. I have no end in view. I do not know how to run minute to minute and hour to hour, solving them by some natural force until they make the

> whole and indivisible mass that you call life. . . .'
>
> (*W*, 87–8)

> 'Listen. There is a sound like the knocking of railway trucks in a siding. That is the happy concatenation of one event following another in our lives. Knock, knock, knock. Must, must, must. Must go, must sleep, must wake, must get up – sober, merciful word which we pretend to revile, which we press tight to our hearts, without which we should be undone. . . .'
>
> (*W*, 158)

> 'What is the solution, I ask myself, and the bridge? How can I reduce these dazzling, these dancing apparitions to one line capable of linking all in one? . . .'
>
> (*W*, 148)

> '"Like" and "like" and "like" – but what is the thing that lies beneath the semblance of the thing? . . .'
>
> (*W*, 110)

> 'I have fifty years, I have sixty years to spend. I have not yet broken into my hoard. This is the beginning. . . .'
>
> (*W*, 37)

F Different Lines

The corollary to the stress on what can be dimly glimpsed 'between the lines' is the possibility of different ones. Dealing with the letter that makes a request for money for the rebuilding of a women's college, Woolf demurs, as in every other case:

> Shall I ask them to rebuild the college on the old lines? Or shall I ask them to rebuild it, but differently? Or shall I ask them to buy rags and petrol and Bryant & May's matches and burn the college to the ground?
>
> (*TG*, 33)

The direction of possible new lines ('but differently') is not clear when that difference can only be marked in relation to the present, unacceptable structure. Hence, for Woolf, the necessary 'failures and fragments' (*CE*, I: 335) of a period of transition onto other lines, and the hesitation as to what kind of 'line' is compatible with a new departure.

Woolf in the end rejects the possibility of a *tabula rasa*, deciding it would not solve the problem to raze the women's college to the ground. With centuries, and ages, of accumulated differentiation and domination, there is no means of suddenly bringing forth an untouched edition of the natural woman or human: Woolf is unsure as to the specificity of difference in the unimaginable state that would precede its imposition. Starting from scratch is impossible; instead, Woolf takes her cues from the script that is already in place. As the essay 'Professions for Women' proclaims the need to kill the Victorian 'Angel in the House', so *Three Guineas* insists on the double onus on women who would be equal members of society to kill the 'lady' (by which Woolf means someone for whom it is deemed inappropriate to be remunerated for her work) and kill the 'woman' (by which Woolf means someone whose duty it is to sacrifice herself to her father).[4] Woolf uses her knowledge of Freud to argue both that the forms of masculine domination have existed since time immemorial, and that they have only just been articulated as such:

> Let us then grope our way amateurishly enough among these very ancient and obscure emotions which we have known ever since the time of Antigone and Ismene and Creon at least: which St Paul himself seems to have felt; but which the Professors have only lately brought to the surface and named 'infantile fixation', 'Oedipus complex', and the rest.
>
> (*TG*, 130)

The problem has now been given a name, put into words: its visibility, beyond the obscurity of what had to be left out before, may now enable it to be demolished, or rewritten in its turn. As to whether the process of analysing and naming will result eventually in the emergence of a new kind of woman (or man), or whether those categories will cease to have the same kind of significance, this is another question that Woolf necessarily leaves open.

G The Incomplete Sentence

> When all the evidence had been given and the lawyers had had their say a silence fell on the hot court, as I began to write my analysis of the evidence and my reasons for my verdict. I wrote away without difficulty, but again and again when I got to the words: '. . . and for these reasons I find the accused guilty of . . . and sentence him to . . .', my hand began to tremble so violently that it was sometimes impossible for me to write legibly and I adjourned for five minutes in order to retire and calm myself sufficiently to complete the sentence (in both senses of the word).[5]

Leonard Woolf's testimony, with its dotted lines to indicate his own hesitation, explicitly brings together the judicial sentence and the written sentence in their joint maintenance of imperial power. The newly feminized Orlando has no regrets for the passing of a life characterized, among other regular practices, by 'sentencing a man to death' (*O*, 100). There is a finality to this which is the exact opposite of what has just been suggested as a more womanly approach, 'continuing the sentence which she had left unfinished the other day' (100).

The dotted line breaks open or leaves incomplete the masculine sentence, imperative and final: the ending to which it proceeds is now postponed, or indeed suspended. Instead of the already known terminus of the line, whether it goes from A to B or from A to Q, the woman's interruption of established communications has thrown into doubt all at once the reasons for the journey, the nature of the destination and even the desirability of predetermined ends for communication.[6] In the matter of literature (who shall tell whose story and how?), in the matter of history (whose history is it, and is the idea of progress and destiny anything more than a comforting myth?) and in the matter of the difference between the differently formed sexes (are their ends compatible, along what new routes are women to divert the train?), lines have now been opened in new directions.

The change of sentence marks both syntax and justice, and takes us back to the mistreated Mrs Brown and to the 'case' of the woman, or woman writer, on trial. Given the man's sentence, the woman is ruled out of order – or rather, she can only be represented as what is left out, as a dotted line whose challenge is that of 'hints and fragments', alluding to something else that cannot be said.

The case of the woman as both judicially accused and syntactically accusative – marked term in relation to the masculine norm, and grammatical object to the masculine subject – implies that her defence and her different sentence could not make sense or be heard as reasonable within the structure as it is: this is the difficulty of her signing her cheque in favour of the standing order of things. But that is also precisely what gives the suggestive power and the greater openness to Woolf's 'between', to the suspended or undecidable 'woman's sentence', and to her continual refusal to come to a conclusion, to complete the sentence. So the last word goes to Bernard in *The Waves*, perhaps a woman writer in Woolf's clothing:[7]

> Behold, then, the blue madonna streaked with tears. This is my funeral service. We have no ceremonies, only private dirges and no conclusions, only violent sensations, each separate. Nothing that has been said meets our case.
>
> (*W*, 105)

Notes

Chapter 1 'We're Getting There': Woolf, Trains and the Destinations of Feminist Criticism

1 Ferdinand de Saussure, *Cours de linguistique générale*, ed. Tullio de Mauro (Paris: Payot, 1984), p. 151. As if to emphasize the question, the English version features the same (or a different) train as not the 8.45, but the 8.25. (*Course in General Linguistics*, trans. Wade Baskin, revised edition with an introduction by Jonathan Culler, London: Fontana, 1974, p. 108).

2 See Melanie Klein, 'The Importance of Symbol Formation in the Development of the Ego' (1930), in *The Selected Melanie Klein*, ed. Juliet Mitchell (Harmondsworth: Penguin, 1986), pp. 102–3.

3 Virginia Woolf, 'Mr Bennett and Mrs Brown' (1924), in *Collected Essays*, I, pp. 319–37. An earlier version of the essay, prompted by criticisms of Woolf by Arnold Bennett, was published the previous year, and this final version was first given as a lecture in Cambridge. For further details see Samuel Hynes, 'The Whole Contention Between Mr Bennett and Mrs Woolf', in *Edwardian Occasions: Essays on English Writing in the Early Twentieth Century* (London: Routledge & Kegan Paul, 1972), pp. 24–38.

4 Michel Foucault describes the multiple implications of a more modern arrangement of the train: 'It's an extraordinary bunch of relationships, the train, since it's something along which you go, it's something too by which you can go from one place to another, and it's also something which goes past' ('Des espaces autres', in *AMC* (*Architecture Mouvement Continuité*), 5 (Oct. 1984), p. 47). The isolation of the compartment before the introduction of corridors gave rise to the often sensationalized interest in 'railway rapes', and to fears and fantasies on the part of passengers, as will become apparent in the context of *Jacob's Room* (ch. 6). For further details on this and every other aspect of the early sociology of the train, see Wolfgang Schivelbusch, *The Railway Journey: Trains and Travel in the 19th Century* (1977), trans. Anselm Hollo (Oxford: Blackwell, 1979).

5 'December, 1910' was the month after the first exhibition of Post-Impressionist paintings opened in London, organized by Roger Fry, and this event itself conceals a further parable of the retrospective marking of an event or a historical break. It was Fry who invented the label 'Post-Impressionist' – an English naming of a French artistic movement, which was then retranslated into French. Further, the 'post' of 'Post-Impressionism' anticipates (or repeats) *avant* (or *post*) *la lettre*, the current discussion of the significance of the 'post' in the terms 'post-structuralism' and especially 'postmodernism'. The postmodern is theorized by Jean-François Lyotard not as what comes after modernity, but as the experimentation or lack of fixity that turns out, retrospectively, to have preceded the establishment of rules and norms of representation in a given period of the history of art. On these issues, see Lyotard, 'Answering the Question: What is Postmodernism?' (1982), trans. Régis Durand, appended to *The Postmodern Condition* (Manchester: Manchester University Press, 1984), pp. 71–84; Geoff Bennington, 'Postal Politics and the Institution of the Nation', forthcoming in Homi Bhabha, ed., *Nation and Narration* (London: Methuen, 1988); and Robert Young, 'Post-Structuralism: The End of Theory', *Oxford Literary Review*, 5, 1–2 (1981), pp. 3–15.

6 A second instance given is that of 'the married life of the Carlyles' (320):

> Bewail the waste, the futility, for him and for her, of the horrible domestic tradition which made it seemly for a woman of genius to spend her time chasing beetles, scouring saucepans, instead of writing books. All human relations have shifted – those between masters and servants, husbands and wives, parents and children. (*CE*, I: 320–1)

Woolf doesn't consider here the possible 'waste' of the 'genius' of a cook, or whether saucepan-scouring and literature are compatible. This is perhaps the point behind Q. D. Leavis's somewhat self-congratulatory remark in her much later review of Woolf's *Three Guineas*: 'I myself . . . have generally had to produce contributions for this review with one hand while actually stirring the pot, or something of that kind, with the other' (*Scrutiny*, 7, 2 (Sept. 1938), p. 210; reprinted in *Virginia Woolf: The Critical Heritage*, ed. Robin Majumdar and Allen McLaurin (London: Routledge & Kegan Paul, 1975), pp. 409–19). 'One' can't help wondering what part Mrs Leavis's husband played in these culinary/textual practices.

7 In 'Modern Fiction', Woolf hints more strongly that the third-class railway carriage may indicate a more serious engagement with novel-writing than that of the men, who in fact are cossetted rather than challenged by the 'material' facts they describe:

> More and more they seem to us, deserting even the well-built villa in the Five Towns, to spend their time in some softly padded

> first-class railway carriage, pressing bells and buttons innumerable; and the destiny to which they travel so luxuriously becomes more and more unquestionably an eternity of bliss spent in the very best hotel in Brighton.
>
> (*CE*, II: 104)

8 Toril Moi, *Sexual/Textual Politics: Feminist Literary Theory* (London, Methuen: New Accents, 1985), p. 8.

Chapter 2 The Trained Mind

1 See *A Room*, pp. 46–8. *Shakespeare's Sisters* is the title of a collection of essays on women poets edited by Sandra M. Gilbert and Susan Gubar (Bloomington: Indiana University Press, 1979).

2 As well as in the *Collected Essays*, 'Professions for Women' appears also in a selection of essays by Woolf on *Women and Writing*, ed. with an introduction by Michèle Barrett (New York: Harcourt Brace Jovanovich, 1979), pp. 57–63. An earlier, much longer version is published in *The Pargiters*: the essay was the basis of Woolf's idea for what became *The Pargiters* and then *The Years*.

3 On the first stage of Woolf's writing against masculine cultural authority, see Christine Froula, 'Out of the Chrysalis: Female Initiation and Female Authority in Virginia Woolf's *The Voyage Out*', *Tulsa Studies in Women's Literature*, 5, 1 (Spring 1986), pp. 63–90.

4 See *A Room*, pp. 59 and 63. The relation between writing and mothering in Woolf is discussed in the final section of this chapter, and at the end of ch. 3.

5 Sandra M. Gilbert and Susan Gubar, *The Madwoman in the Attic: The Woman Writer and the Nineteenth-Century Literary Imagination* (New Haven: Yale University Press, 1979).

6 Elaine Showalter, *A Literature of Their Own: British Women Novelists from Brontë to Lessing* (London: Virago, 1978). Showalter's tenth chapter is entitled 'Virginia Woolf and the Flight into Androgyny'.

7 See, for example, Barbara Smith, 'Toward a Black Feminist Criticism', in Elaine Showalter, ed., *The New Feminist Criticism* (London: Virago, 1985), pp. 177–210, and also in Judith Newton and Deborah Rosenfelt, eds, *Feminist Criticism and Social Change* (London: Methuen, 1985), pp. 3–18; Bonnie Zimmerman, 'What Has Never Been: An Overview of Lesbian Feminist Criticism', in Showalter, ed., pp. 200–24, also in Gayle Greene and Coppélia Kahn, eds, *Making A Difference: Feminist Literary Criticism* (London: Methuen, 1985), pp. 177–210.

8 Published originally as an 'Introductory Letter to Margaret Llewellyn Davies' in Margaret Llewellyn Davies, ed., *Life As We Have Known It* by Co-operative Working Women (London: Hogarth Press, 1931), pp. xv–xxxix; reprinted as 'Memories of a Working Women's Guild', *Collected Essays*, vol. IV, pp. 134–48.

9 'Indeed, I would venture to guess that Anon, who wrote so many poems without signing them, was often a woman' (*ROO*, 48). In the Granada edition, 'signing' is misprinted as 'singing', which suggests an inverse relationship between the two: even more anonymous than Anon, who wrote without signing, are the women who sang without writing, even anonymously. The very next sentence continues: 'It was a woman Edward Fitzgerald, I think, suggested who made the ballads and the folk-songs, crooning them to her children, beguiling her spinning with them, or the length of the winter's night' (*ROO*, 48). Maria DiBattista interprets the folksongs of Anon in Woolf as her vision of a maternal poetry anterior to the polemical forms of masculine history and literature. See *Virginia Woolf's Major Novels: The Fables of Anon* (New Haven: Yale University Press, 1980), especially pp. 228–34.

10 See *The Pelican Freud Library* (Harmondsworth: Penguin, 1973–87), 'Female Sexuality' (1931), vol. 7, p. 372, and *The Question of Lay Analysis* (1926), vol. 15, p. 313.

11 Hélène Cixous, 'Tancrède continue' (1983), in *Entre l'écriture* (Paris: éditions des femmes, 1986), p. 165. Short extracts from the work of Cixous and others, including Luce Irigaray and Julia Kristeva, are translated in Elaine Marks and Isabelle de Courtivron, eds, *New French Feminisms* (Amherst: University of Massachussetts Press, 1980). *La Jeune née* (1975), a joint text written with Catherine Clément, has now been translated by Betsy Wing as *The Newly Born Woman* (Manchester: Manchester University Press, 1986).

12 Makiko Minow-Pinkney analyses the implications and possibilities of this dilemma in a book which draws fully on the theoretical insights of French feminist theory. In *Virginia Woolf and the Problem of the Subject* (Brighton: Harvester Press, 1987), she reads Woolf's oeuvre as an anticipation of Julia Kristeva's theorization of the possible emergence of a new, 'post-individualist' subjectivity from the greater openness of the maternal/feminine 'semiotic', prior to the imposition of the symbolic order.

13 *Speculum of the Other Woman* has been translated by Gillian C. Gill (Ithaca: Cornell University Press, 1985).

14 Nancy Topping Bazin, *Virginia Woolf and the Androgynous Vision* (New Brunswick: Rutgers University Press, 1973), p. 3. Other books which deal with the notion of androgyny in Woolf include Carolyn G. Heilbrun, *Towards Androgyny: Aspects of Male and Female in Literature* (1964; rpt. London: Victor Gollancz, 1973); Herbert Marder, *Feminism and Art: A Study of Virginia Woolf* (Chicago: University of Chicago Press, 1968); and Phyllis Rose, *Woman of Letters: A Life Of Virginia Woolf* (London: Routledge & Kegan Paul, 1978).

15 Showalter, *A Literature*, p. 288.

Chapter 3 Orlando's Vacillation

1 For the first model, see Julia Kristeva, 'Women's Time' (1979), trans. Alice Jardine and Harry Blake, *Signs*, 7, 1 (Fall 1981), pp. 13–35, also

in Toril Moi, ed., *The Kristeva Reader* (Oxford: Blackwell, 1986); for the second, see Ann Douglas, *The Feminization of American Culture* (1977; rpt. New York: Avon, 1978). The second approach equates femininity with passivity and superficiality, and sees this association as cultural: while accepting the negative connotations of both, it does not identify women with what is culturally taken to be feminine. The first approach sees the social construction of femininity as inseparable from psychic formations, and considers the effects on society and on forms of subjectivity of the various types of feminist challenge to patriarchal time.

2 The 'and/or' of *Orlando* is noted also by Françoise Defromont in *Virginia Woolf: Vers la maison de lumière* (Paris: éditions des femmes, 1985), p. 209, and by Hélène and Jean-Michel Rabaté, in 'Orlando amoroso', *Europe*, no. 676/677 (août–septembre 1985), pp. 26–35. In view of the subject matter of *Orlando*, it seemed reasonable to suppose that the latter article was written by a single author (one surname, masculine and feminine first names). However, Jean-Michel Rabaté, from whom I sought enlightenment on this point, assures me that such suspicions are unfounded: there are two authors of two distinct sexes.

3 Freud, 'Femininity' (1933), in *New Introductory Lectures on Psychoanalysis*, vol. 2 of *Pelican Freud*, p. 146.

4 'Unhesitating certainty' and first or anonymous meetings are linked also by a buried street connection. The 'obvious' is etymologically 'what crosses your path', *ob viam*, and is close in sense to the word 'trivial', literally 'where three roads (*viae*) meet', hence 'commonplace'. Part of Woolf's strategy, as in the questioning in *A Room* of 'the difference of value' and the trivialization of the feminine, is to take a second look at what is so 'obvious' as the difference of the sexes: to suggest that 'the first distinction you make' may be the most questionable precisely because it is the first, and therefore sets the terms for all subsequent distinctions: it is so automatic as to seem natural.

Elsewhere, and notably in *Jacob's Room*, as we shall see, Woolf looks twice, or looks again, at the seemingly 'obvious' readings of everyday encounters in public places; 'Mr Bennett and Mrs Brown' is specifically concerned with the lack of certainty and lurking strangeness in an ordinary railway journey.

5 'Here she tossed her foot impatiently, and happened to show an inch or two of calf. A sailor on the mast, who happened to look down at the moment, started so violently that he missed his footing and only saved himself by the skin of his teeth. . . . "A pox on them!" she said, realizing for the first time what, in other circumstances, she would have been taught as a child, that is to say, the sacred responsibilities of womanhood' (*O*, 98).

6 This quotation forms the starting point of the first chapter, 'Reading Woman (Reading)', of Mary Jacobus's *Reading Woman* (London: Methuen, 1986). In this analysis, I am drawing on recent work in film theory as well as literary theory which uses the psychoanalytic concept

of masquerade derived from Joan Riviere's article 'Womanliness as a Masquerade' (1929), reprinted in Victor Burgin, James Donald and Cora Kaplan, eds, *Formations of Fantasy* (London: Methuen, 1986). See further Mary Ann Doane, 'Film and the Masquerade: Theorising the Female Spectator', *Screen*, 23, 3–4 (September–October 1982), pp. 74–87.

7 In her diaries, Woolf frequently compares her books to babies, and frequently compares herself with her sister Vanessa Bell, who is both a mother and an artist. For example: 'How odd to think that I have given the world something that the world enjoys – I refer to the Manchester Guardian – Orlando is recognized for the masterpiece that it is. The Times does not mention Nessa's pictures. Yet, she said last night, I have spent a long time over one of them. Then I think to myself, So I have something, instead of children, & fall comparing our lives' (*D*, 3: 217 (Friday 4 January, 1929)). (A footnote makes it clear that 'the masterpiece it is' is in fact a quotation from the newspaper.)

8 See Defromont, *Virginia Woolf*, p. 221.

Chapter 4 Getting to Q: Sexual Lines in *To the Lighthouse*

1 Jacques Lacan, 'The agency of the letter in the unconscious' (1957), in *Ecrits*, trans. Alan Sheridan (London: Tavistock, 1977), p. 152.

2 Ernest Jones, *Sigmund Freud: Life and Work*, vol. I (London: Hogarth Press, 1956), p. 14.

3 Freud, *Three Essays on the Theory of Sexuality* (1905), Pelican Freud, vol. 7, p. 121.

4 Details of the Hogarth Press's publications of translations of Freud in the twenties and of the later negotiations to publish the Standard Edition, chiefly translated by James Strachey, are to be found in Leonard Woolf's autobiography, particularly the fourth volume, *Downhill All the Way: An Autobiography of the Years 1919–1939* (London: Hogarth Press, 1962), pp. 163–8, and the fifth, *The Journey Not the Arrival Matters: An Autobiography of the Years 1939–1969* (New York: Harcourt, Brace & World, 1970), pp. 117–18.

5 Freud, 'Femininity' (1933), *Pelican Freud*, vol 2, p. 168.

6 This, incidentally, would show up another side to the harmonious view of the couple getting into the taxi in *A Room of One's Own*.

7 In two ways in particular the girl has to accomplish a more difficult journey: by changing the sex of the object of love (from female to male: the boy has only to substitute another woman for the mother) and by changing the chief site of erotic arousal (from clitoris to vagina). Initially, there is no difference in the sexuality of boys and girls; it is only after the girl has understood the meaning of sexual difference – an understanding which Freud mythically attaches to sightings of the genitals of the other sex – that (in the 'normal' course of development) she regards herself as lacking and gives up the forms of sexuality that

are now, retroactively, identified as masculine. In addition to the texts cited above, see further on this 'Some Psychical Consequences of the Anatomical Distinction Between the Sexes' (1925) and 'Female Sexuality' (1931), both in *Pelican Freud*, vol. 7.

Two recent studies of *To the Lighthouse* look at Woolf's undermining of the Freudian scenario of feminine development. See Margaret Homans, 'Mothers and Daughters in Virginia Woolf's Victorian Novel', in *Bearing the Word: Language and Female Experience in Nineteenth-Century Women's Writing* (Chicago: University of Chicago Press, 1986), pp. 277–88; and Gayatri C. Spivak, 'Unmaking and Making in *To the Lighthouse*', in Sally McConnell-Ginet, Ruth Borker and Nelly Furman, eds, *Women and Language in Literature and Society* (New York: Praeger, 1980), pp. 310–27. Other suggestive work includes Anne Juranville, 'La Figure de la mère chez Virginia Woolf', *Psychanalyse à l'université*, 7, 26 (mars 1982), pp. 219–49; and Françoise Defromont, *Virginia Woolf*, especially pages 100–27. Both these studies are written from a Lacanian point of view.

8 On the temporality of *To the Lighthouse*, see the classic final chapter, 'The Brown Stocking', of Erich Auerbach's *Mimesis: The Representation of Reality in Western Literature* (1946), trans. Willard R. Trask (Princeton: Princeton University Press, 1953), pp. 525–3. On narrative and temporality in Woolf's novels generally, see the two final chapters of J. Hillis Miller, *Fiction and Repetition: Seven English Novels* (Cambridge: Harvard University Press, 1982), on *Mrs Dalloway* and *Between the Acts*; and Paul Ricoeur, *Temps et récit*, (Paris: Seuil), vol. II (1984), pp. 152–67, and vol. III (1985), pp. 184–202, also on *Mrs Dalloway*.

9 For two perspectives on the idea of a 'feminine' quality of texts which subvert the realist norm, see Julia Kristeva, 'From One Identity to an Other' (1975), in her *Desire in Language: A Semiotic Approach to Literatue and Art* (Oxford: Blackwell, 1980), ed. Leon S. Roudiez, pp. 124–47, and Hélène Cixous, *The Newly Born Woman.*

Chapter 5 Thinking Forward Through Mrs Dalloway's Daughter

1 See chapter 2, n. 2.

2 Charlotte Brontë, *Jane Eyre* (1847; rpt. Harmondsworth: Penguin, 1984), p. 140.

3 Ibid., pp. 140–41.

4 Charlotte Brontë, *Villette* (1853; rpt. Harmondsworth: Penguin, 1981), p. 109.

5 Ibid., pp. 117–18.

6 Ibid, p. 107.

7 Difference of class rather than community of sex seems to come to the fore in Woolf's portrayals of 'Unfortunate Julia! wetting her pen in bitterness, and leaving her shoe laces untied' (*JR*, 103), and (through Katherine Hilbery's eyes) of the odd enthusiasts in the office of a

feminist organization (*ND*, 74–82). And this is perhaps the place to mention also the awkwardness of Woolf's occasional refusal of a relationship between literature and politics, giving support to the myth of Bloomsbury elitism. In 'Mr Bennett and Mrs Brown', for instance, one of the objections to the Edwardians is what she perceives as an imperative to action in their novels: 'In order to complete them it seems necessary to do something – to join a society or, more desperately, to write a cheque. . . . [The Edwardians] were interested in something outside. Their books, then, were incomplete as books, and required that the reader should finish them, actively and practically, for himself' (*CE* I, 326–7).

8 Elizabeth Abel, 'Narrative Structure(s) and Female Development: The Case of *Mrs Dalloway*', in Elizabeth Abel, Marianne Hirsch, and Elizabeth Langland, eds, *The Voyage In: Fictions of Female Development* (Hanover: University Press of New England, 1983), p. 171.

9 The Peter Walsh/Richard Dalloway difference may be compared with Woolf's story in *A Sketch of the Past* of the habitual family marking of the difference between her mother's two husbands, 'her two incongruous choices' (*MB*, 105). The first, Herbert Duckworth, as mentioned below in ch. 6, figured as the legendary Greek hero; in relation to him, 'the gaunt bearded man' (*MB*, 105), Leslie Stephen, was 'in every way the opposite' (*MB*, 106).

10 Paul Ricoeur, *Temps et récit*, vol. II, *La configuration dans le récit de fiction* (ch. 4, n. 8), especially pp. 158–9.

11 Bernard might seem to be the exception here: 'For I am more selves than Neville thinks' (*W*, 60); 'With them I am many-sided' (*W*, 78). But his selves are not so much disparate and incompatible as personae presented in company; and this multiplicity is in fact the idiosyncratic feature which differentiates him from the others: 'To be myself (I note) I need the illumination of other people's eyes and therefore cannot be entirely sure what is myself. The authentics, like Louis, like Rhoda, exist most completely in solitude' (*W*, 78).

12 The continuity here between the sealing matter and what it covers over should be contrasted with a different use of the same imagery in 'A Sketch of the Past'. See chapter 6, p. 109.

13 Peter's internal divisions and his non-identification with the British Establishment detract from his masculinity, in so far as perfect masculinity is perfect adjustment (there is no jar within an entirely 'British breast' (*MD*,19), or between it and its equally British outside). This appropriately gives rise to 'the sense that he was not altogether manly' (*MD*, 138).

Chapter 6 Jacob's Type

1 See E. M. Forster, *Aspects of the Novel* (1927; rpt. Harmondsworth: Penguin, 1962), pp. 75–89.

2 Judy Little explores this aspect in '*Jacob's Room* as Comedy: Woolf's Parodic *Bildungsroman*', in Jane Marcus, ed., *New Feminist Essays on Virginia Woolf* (London: Macmillan, 1981), pp. 105–24.
3 Woolf's fascination with and continual exploration of the city in her writing has been most thoroughly investigated in Susan Squier, *Virginia Woolf and London* (Chapel Hill: University of North Carolina Press, 1985).
4 On the 'sketch' in Woolf, see James Naremore, *The World Without a Self: Virginia Woolf and the Novel* (New Haven: Yale University Press, 1973), pp. 101–3.
5 Compare with this use of sealing imagery the passage of *Mrs Dalloway* discussed in chapter 5, p. 94.
6 For more on Woolf's metaphors of system and network, see Perry Meisel, *The Absent Father: Virginia Woolf and Walter Pater* (New Haven: Yale University Press, 1980).

Chapter 7 Things

1 Compare Leonard Woolf, *Beginning Again: An Autobiography of the Years 1911–1918* (London: Hogarth Press, 1964), p. 64:

> In the 50 years since we had Asham House, the physical basis of life in the English countryside has been revolutionized. Conditions in Sussex in 1912 were pretty primitive, and our daily life was probably nearer that of Chaucer's than of the modern man with water from the main, electricity, gas, cars, motor buses, telephone, wireless.

This practice of connecting historical change to changes in 'things' is frequent in Woolf's diary, too, and she often marks the change as affecting the very forms of language and thought: new things are connected to new ways of conceptualizing the world and the person's relation to it. On the car, for example, following the Woolfs' acquisition of a second-hand Singer in the summer of 1927:

> This is a great opening up in our lives. One may go to Bodiam, to Arundel, explore the Chichester downs, expand that curious thing, the map of the world in ones mind.
>
> (*D*, 3: 147)

> All images are now tinged with driving a motor. Here I think of letting my engine work, with my clutch out.
>
> (*D*, 3: 149)

2 See below, ch. 8.
3 See Roland Barthes, 'Introduction to the Structuralist Analysis of Narratives' (1966), trans. Stephen Heath in *Image Music Text* (London: Fontana, 1977), pp. 79–124.

4 The return of characters to England after a number of years in the outposts of Empire is often a device for Woolf to introduce a character's comparison of 'now' and 'then'. Peter Walsh in *Mrs Dalloway* comes back to London after five years in India and gives his impressions of a difference represented in terms of greater public openness. This is exemplified by a letter to the paper about 'water closets', by girls putting on make-up in public, and by couples 'carrying on quite openly' when not engaged to be married (*MD*, 65). The implied progressive narrative of a gradual removal of conventional inhibitions on natural forms of physical expression only awaiting their release is akin to Woolf's own account, in 'Old Bloomsbury' (*MB*, 183–207), of the lifting of Victorian taboos for members of her generation.

Beginning Again, the title of the third volume of Leonard Woolf's autobiography (London: Hogarth Press, 1964), refers to his return to England in 1911 after seven years as a civil servant in Ceylon. He stresses the difference made by what he found to be the extension of 'intimacy . . . both personal and intellectual' (33). In 1904:

> It would have been inconceivable that I should have called Lytton's or Thoby's sisters by their Christian names. The social significance of using Christian instead of surnames and of kissing instead of shaking hands is curious. . . . It was this feeling of greater intimacy and freedom, of the sweeping away of formalities and barriers, which I found so new and so exhilarating in 1911. To have discussed some subjects or to have called a (sexual) spade a spade in the presence of Miss Strachey or Miss Stephen would seven years before have been unimaginable.
>
> (Ibid., p. 35)

Of course, the concept of 'a (sexual) spade', a euphemism to illustrate the release from euphemisms, would immediately give the lie to the linguistic emancipation it is supposed to prove – unless evidence has been dug up to show that Leonard Woolf's erotic preoccupations were unusually horticultural.

5 Woolf's metaphors in *Mrs Dalloway* (19) and *Moments of Being* (143) of the self 'sealed' with wax that may come unstuck were discussed in chapters 5 and 6, pp. 94 and 109.

Chapter 8 Orlando's Undoing

1 The relationship between forms of language, history and subjectivity is constantly explored in Woolf's novels. *Orlando* is unique in that its premise of a subject running parallel with history makes it possible to raise the questions of biographical and historical reconstruction in tandem. *Between the Acts* is in one sense the closest to *Orlando*, because there too, as I shall describe in ch. 9, the relation between historical periods and forms of subjectivity is posed, and via a history presented in the form of a series of literary pastiches. In *Between the Acts*, the

undoing of subjectivity and of history is taken at the level of the breakdown of language and form much more than in *Orlando*, where the relatively smooth sequences and conventional structure throw into relief the undermining that is going on in every other respect.

For more on the issues of historical narrative raised in this chapter, see Michel Foucault, *Les Mots et les choses* (1966), trans. *The Order of Things* (London: Tavistock, 1970), and *L'Archéologie du savoir* (1969), trans. *The Archaeology of Knowledge* (London: Tavistock, 1972).

2 The term 'photographic realism', where the camera provides the modern, mechanical analogy for the new ideal of a scientifically infallible objectivity in literarature, was chiefly associated with writers also known as 'naturalists'. Emile Zola is most often cited as the exemplar of this tendency. In England, the label was attached to novelists like those Woolf denigrates in her essays as 'materialists'. There is this, for example, from the biography of Roger Fry: 'Why, he demanded, was there no English author who took his art seriously? Why were they all engrossed in childish problems of photographic representation?' (*RF*, 164).

3 For this playing 'on the double temporality of story and narration', see further Gérard Genette, *Figures III* (Paris: Seuil, 1972), ch. 5, p. 244. Genette characterizes this type of transgression of narrative levels, when it is 'as if the narration were contemporaneous with the story and had to fill up its dead time', as 'narrative metalepsis'.

4 See Andrew Marvell, 'The Garden': 'Annihilating all that's made/To a green thought in a green shade' (lines 47f.). Looking in another direction, it has been pointed out to me that I have been typing this text on something called a 'green screen'.

Chapter 9 Partings

1 Leonard Woolf, *The Journey Not the Arrival Matters*, pp. 9–10.

2 In view of the theatrical setting of *Between the Acts*, the French word for 'rehearsal', *répétition*, suggests further ambiguities: the *répétition* is what comes before, rather than repeating, the 'real' performance; the performance can only take place after it has been 'repeated'.

3 The 'kitchen change' might be linked to Woolf's suggestion in 'Mr Bennett and Mrs Brown' that the change in human nature is best exemplified by 'the rise of the cook'; and also to a footnote in *Three Guineas* which uses the difference of class between mistress and maid (via the position of the maid as her mistress's chaperone in the city) to underline the contradictions of the double standard:

> We have only to consider the hours she waited in cloak rooms, the acres she toiled in picture galleries, the miles she trudged along West End pavements to conclude that if Lizzie's day is now almost over, it was in its day a long one. Let us hope that the thought that she was putting into practice the commands laid

> down by St Paul in his Letters to Titus and the Corinthians was a support; and the knowledge that she was doing her utmost to deliver her mistress's body intact to her master a solace. Even so in the weakness of the flesh and in the darkness of the beetle-haunted basement she must sometimes have bitterly reproached St Paul on the one hand for his chastity, and the gentlemen of Piccadilly on the other for their lust. It is much to be regretted that no lives of maids, from which a more fully documented account could be constructed, are to be found in the *Dictionary of National Biography*.
>
> (*TG*, 165–6)

As in *To the Lighthouse*, the time of the repeated 'day' comes to the fore, through the interminability of the maid's ('it was in its day a long one'), and the alleged approaching end of this kind of existence ('if Lizzie's day is now almost over'), and suggests the marking of an event by the end of a form of daily life: 'in its day' points to something as both past and quotidian, like the 'Things that were . . .' of Roger Fry's mother.

4 'My mother does say I am his son, but I don't know myself. After all, no-one can be sure of his own father' (Homer, *The Odyssey*, Book I, lines 215–16).

5 For an analysis of other 'mirror identification' passages in Woolf, see Perry Meisel, *The Absent Father*, pp. 167–73.

6 I am drawing here on recent accounts of 'the postmodern', as a hypothetical new post-war period differentiated from the past by its psychic and cultural depthlessness and fragmentation of parts without unity or centre; and/or as that which puts in question the very possibility of periodization (including and especially the period of postmodernism). See for example Andreas Huyssen, *After the Great Divide: Modernism, Mass Culture, Postmodernism* (Bloomington: Indiana University Press, 1986); Fredric Jameson, 'Postmodernism, or the Cultural Logic of Late Capitalism', *New Left Review*, 146 (July–August 1984), 53–92; Jean-François Lyotard, *The Postmodern Condition* (1979), trans. Geoff Bennington and Brian Massumi (Manchester: Manchester University Press, 1984), and *Le Postmoderne expliqué aux enfants* (Paris: Galilée, 1986). See also ch. 1, n. 5, above.

7 Jacques Derrida, *Of Grammatology* (1967), trans. Gayatri Chakravorty Spivak (Baltimore: John Hopkins University Press, 1976), p. 5. A similar configuration occurs at the end of Derrida's essay 'Structure, Sign and Play in the Discourse of the Human Sciences' (1966), in *Writing and Difference*, trans. Alan Bass (London: Routledge & Kegan Paul, 1978), p. 293.

Chapter 10 The Dotted Line

1 Woolf planned what became *The Years* as an 'essay–novel' in which chapters of fiction would alternate with explanatory essays on the

sociohistorical background. Manuscripts of early drafts in this form have now been edited by Mitchell A. Leaska, and published as *The Pargiters: The Novel–Essay Portion of 'The Years'* (New York: Harcourt Brace Jovanovich, 1977).

2 The ambiguities of this passage in *A Room* are analysed in more detail in the section of ch. 2 entitled 'Sentences', pp. 28–30.

3 In *The Absent Father* (pp. 229–33), Perry Meisel analyses the rhetorical complicity in this text between Woolf's anti-patriarchal 'weapons' and the militaristic order they are designed to overthrow.

4 See *Three Guineas*, pp. 133–4. Other, more problematic implications of Woolf's rhetoric of violence against female figures are discussed in the final sections of ch. 2, in relation to the projected murder of the Angel and the three times repeated threat of a 'fatal' result for writers who 'think of their sex' (*ROO*, 99). There is also the difficult moment in *Three Guineas* when she seems to suggest that the word 'feminist', now redundant because women have acquired the right to earn a living, should be ceremoniously burned as 'a word without a meaning . . . a dead word, a corrupt word' (*TG*, 101). Even if we allow that there is irony here, in view of the comments elsewhere on the small number of women who have actually entered the professions, and on other forms of inequality than the professional, on the next page 'the word "feminist"' is made analogous to two totally unexpected, and alarming, comrades: 'What could be more fitting than to write more dead words, more corrupt words, upon more sheets of paper and burn them – the words, Tyrant, Dictator, for example? But, alas, those words are not yet obsolete' (*TG*, 102). (See also p. 80.)

This is also perhaps the place to mention that Woolf's advocacy of wages for childrearing in this text (*TG*, 111) assumes that it is women who will be earning them.

5 Leonard Woolf, *Sowing: An Autobiography of the Years 1880–1904* (1960; rpt. London: Hogarth Press, 1962), p. 81. The passage refers to the period immediately after this, when Woolf was working for the British government in Ceylon. Interestingly, the double hesitation over the 'sentence' is linked two pages later to a difficulty with signing on the dotted line in public: 'The tremor in my hands has always tended to become extreme if I have to sign my name before other people, particularly on cheques or similar documents'.

6 The movement from A to G in this chapter is meant to echo the ambivalence of the keyboard analogy of a repeated and partial alphabetical sequence in *To the Lighthouse*, discussed in ch. 4, p. 65.

7 'For this is not one life; nor do I always know if I am man or woman, Bernard or Neville, Louis, Susan, Jinny or Rhoda – so strange is the contact of one with another' (*W*, 190).

Index